ineering ncil
3|9|2016
TIMOTHY BROWN
MEng CEng MBCS ACGI
Chartered Engineer
Registrant 621166 of the Engineering Council

Learning Game Physics with Bullet Physics and OpenGL

Practical 3D physics simulation experience with modern feature-rich graphics and physics APIs

Chris Dickinson

[PACKT] open source ✽
PUBLISHING   community experience distilled

BIRMINGHAM - MUMBAI

Learning Game Physics with Bullet Physics and OpenGL

First published: October 2013

Production Reference: 1181013

Published by Packt Publishing Ltd.
Livery Place
35 Livery Street
Birmingham B3 2PB, UK.

ISBN 978-1-78328-187-9

www.packtpub.com

Cover Image by Abhishek Pandey (abhishek.pandey1210@gmail.com)

Credits

Author
Chris Dickinson

Reviewers
Marco Altomonte

Ian Voyce

Acquisition Editor
Vinay Argekar

Commissioning Editor
Poonam Jain

Technical Editor
Shali Sasidharan

Project Coordinator
Amigya Khurana

Proofreader
Lesley Harrison

Indexer
Monica Ajmera Mehta

Graphics
Ronak Dhruv

Yuvraj Mannari

Abhinash Sahu

Production Coordinator
Nitesh Thakur

Cover Work
Nitesh Thakur

About the Author

Chris Dickinson grew up in England with a strong passion for science, mathematics, and, in particular, video games. He received his Master's degree in Physics with Electronics from the University of Leeds in 2005, and then left for California to work in scientific research in the heart of Silicon Valley. Finding that career path unsuitable, he began working in software testing and automation.

For years, he attempted to unravel the magic behind video games and 3D worlds through modding and level design, and was mostly self taught in software development and design. But, realizing that he needed proper tutelage and a stronger grasp of the fundamentals, if he ever wanted to build these complex applications himself, he decided to undertake a Bachelor's in Game and Simulation Programming while simultaneously working full time. He earned his second degree in early 2013 and continues his career in software development/test automation while simultaneously developing independent game projects in his spare time.

I would like to thank my wonderful wife and best friend, Jamie, for always being supportive, and eager to help; not to mention, for putting up with me and my never-ending list of projects and erratic work schedule. I'd also like to extend a warm thanks to the good folks at Blizzard Entertainment for bringing us together through a shared addiction to World of Warcraft. Also, my friends, for their constant pestering and high expectations of me to get things done, and, of course, my family for unleashing me on the world and giving me all of the possibilities I was able to explore. To have learned, lived, and loved so much in such a short space of time is only thanks to the opportunities and motivation given to me by all of you.

About the Reviewers

Marco Altomonte is working for Milestone S.r.l. on the graphics engine used in multiplatform video games, such as MotoGP, World Rally Championship, and SBK.

He developed the XNA game, RC Racing 360, published on Microsoft Live Marketplace for Xbox 360.

He worked for ALTAIR Robotics Lab in Robotics and Physics Simulation department. He developed a **GPGPU (General-purpose computing on graphics processing units)** soft body simulator with haptic feedback for a surgeon training software.

He authored *Simulation of deformable environment with haptic feedback on GPU*, published in *Proceedings 3959-3964, IROS 2008: International Conference on Intelligent Robots and Systems*.

Ian Voyce is a developer with a broad range of experience gained over many years in the software industry. He has worked for a variety of clients from advertising agencies to investment banks, as well as made several independent releases to the Apple AppStore.

He has a background in creative computing and user experience with in-depth technical knowledge and a professional specialism in quantitative development. He tries to find the time to combine his favorite pursuits of blogging (at www.voyce.com), creating and playing games, and spending quality of time with his two daughters.

www.PacktPub.com

Support files, eBooks, discount offers and more

You might want to visit www.PacktPub.com for support files and downloads related to your book.

Did you know that Packt offers eBook versions of every book published, with PDF and ePub files available? You can upgrade to the eBook version at www.PacktPub.com and as a print book customer, you are entitled to a discount on the eBook copy. Get in touch with us at service@packtpub.com for more details.

At www.PacktPub.com, you can also read a collection of free technical articles, sign up for a range of free newsletters and receive exclusive discounts and offers on Packt books and eBooks.

http://PacktLib.PacktPub.com

Do you need instant solutions to your IT questions? PacktLib is Packt's online digital book library. Here, you can access, read and search across Packt's entire library of books.

Why Subscribe?

- Fully searchable across every book published by Packt
- Copy and paste, print and bookmark content
- On demand and accessible via web browser

Free Access for Packt account holders

If you have an account with Packt at www.PacktPub.com, you can use this to access PacktLib today and view nine entirely free books. Simply use your login credentials for immediate access.

Table of Contents

Preface

Modern 3D graphics and game physics can seem like complex and confusing elements of game development from the outside, but this book will reveal what's going on under the hood of two modern and feature-rich graphics and physics APIs: OpenGL and Bullet physics. After you finish this book, you'll be armed with a wealth of knowledge to tackle some of the more advanced aspects of game graphics and physics going forward.

This book can't hope to show all of the concepts and intricacies of modern physics and 3D graphical rendering, but it will cover all of the fundamentals in enough detail to let you hit the ground running when you take on future challenges. And if those challenges involve building an application with the Bullet physics library, then all the better, because you will also learn exactly how this library works from the ground up and help you focus on only the important parts of what you need to know about simulating game physics.

What this book covers

Chapter 1, Building a Game Application, identifies the files and libraries required to incorporate the FreeGLUT and Bullet libraries into a starter project, and how to build an application layer to communicate with the operating system.

Chapter 2, Rendering and User Input, introduces some core 3D rendering concepts, implements our very first graphical object complete with lighting and color, and adds user input to our application to control the scene's camera.

Chapter 3, Physics Initialization, introduces the essential concepts of Bullet and the core objects required to build our physics simulation, and attaches a physical rigid body to our graphical object, observing how physics and graphics work together to create a simulated world.

Chapter 4, Object Management and Debug Rendering, runs through some essential refactoring of the code in order to better handle multiple objects, and adds debug rendering to our scene, enabling us to visualize essential information from the physics engine.

Chapter 5, Raycasting and Constraints, introduces the flexibility of raycasting in finding, creating, and destroying objects, and will show us how to add limitations to the motion of our physical objects, allowing even greater control of the objects in our simulation.

Chapter 6, Events, Triggers, and Explosions, implements a simple and effective method for extracting collision event information out of Bullet, builds a basic trigger volume that can trigger these events, and demonstrates the power of these features by simulating an explosion.

Chapter 7, Collision Shapes, introduces several new types of physical object and methods for rendering them from basic spheres and cylinders to shapes built from any arbitrary list of points.

Chapter 8, Collision Filtering, implements a means of separating unwanted contact responses through a simple filtering method.

Chapter 9, Soft Body Dynamics, provides a brief look at complex soft body shapes and their requirements, and implements one into our scene.

What you need for this book

An intermediate level of understanding of the C++ language is required for this book as it is not a programming tutorial, but rather an exploration of existing APIs that have already been through countless hours of development. Also, a working knowledge of 3D mathematics is essential as it is assumed that you have a good understanding of concepts such as vectors and matrices, and how they can be used to represent a 3D space.

A C++ compiler is necessary to compile the book's source code applications. This book uses Visual Studio as a reference, and the source code comes with the Visual Studio solution files. Note that Visual Studio Express can be downloaded from the Microsoft website for free, and it has all of the features necessary to compile the source code and complete this book.

Finally, the Bullet and FreeGLUT libraries will be used, but since they are open source software, they can be freely downloaded from their project websites, which will be explained in *Chapter 1, Building a Game Application*.

Who this book is for

If you're a beginner or intermediate programmer with a basic understanding of 3D mathematics and you want a stronger foundation in 3D graphics and physics, then this book is perfect for you! *Learning Game Physics with Bullet Physics and OpenGL* will take you through a series of straightforward tutorials until you have a strong foundation in both APIs. You'll even learn some of the fundamental concepts in 3D mathematics, and software design that lies beneath them both, discovering some techniques and tricks in graphics and physics that you will use in any game development project.

Conventions

In this book, you will find a number of styles of text that distinguish between different kinds of information. Here are some examples of these styles, and an explanation of their meaning.

Code words in text are shown as follows: "The glutKeyboardFunc and glutKeyboardUpFunc functions are called when FreeGLUT detects that a keyboard key has been pressed down or up, respectively."

A block of code is set as follows:

```
int main(int argc, char** argv)
{
  BulletOpenGLApplication demo;
  return glutmain(argc, argv, 1024, 768, "Introduction to Game
 Physics with Bullet Physics and OpenGL", &demo);
}
```

When we wish to draw your attention to a particular part of a code block, the relevant lines or items are set in bold:

```
DrawBox(btVector3(1, 1, 1), btVector3(1.0f, 0.2f, 0.2f));
```

New terms and **important words** are shown in bold. Words that you see on the screen, in menus or dialog boxes for example, appear in the text like this: "To run a different project, right-click on one of the projects, and select **Set as StartUp Project**."

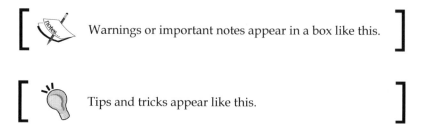

Warnings or important notes appear in a box like this.

Tips and tricks appear like this.

Reader feedback

Feedback from our readers is always welcome. Let us know what you think about this book—what you liked or may have disliked. Reader feedback is important for us to develop titles that you really get the most out of.

To send us general feedback, simply send an e-mail to feedback@packtpub.com, and mention the book title through the subject of your message.

If there is a topic that you have expertise in and you are interested in either writing or contributing to a book, see our author guide on www.packtpub.com/authors.

Customer support

Now that you are the proud owner of a Packt book, we have a number of things to help you to get the most from your purchase.

Downloading the example code

You can download the example code files for all Packt books you have purchased from your account at http://www.packtpub.com. If you purchased this book elsewhere, you can visit http://www.packtpub.com/support and register to have the files e-mailed directly to you.

Downloading the color images of this book

We also provide you a PDF file that has color images of the screenshots/diagrams used in this book. The color images will help you better understand the changes in the output. You can download this file from: `http://www.packtpub.com/sites/default/files/downloads/1879OS_ColoredImages.pdf`.

Errata

Although we have taken every care to ensure the accuracy of our content, mistakes do happen. If you find a mistake in one of our books—maybe a mistake in the text or the code—we would be grateful if you would report this to us. By doing so, you can save other readers from frustration and help us improve subsequent versions of this book. If you find any errata, please report them by visiting `http://www.packtpub.com/support`, selecting your book, clicking on the **errata submission form** link, and entering the details of your errata. Once your errata are verified, your submission will be accepted and the errata will be uploaded to our website, or added to any list of existing errata, under the Errata section of that title.

Piracy

Piracy of copyright material on the Internet is an ongoing problem across all media. At Packt, we take the protection of our copyright and licenses very seriously. If you come across any illegal copies of our works, in any form, on the Internet, please provide us with the location address or website name immediately so that we can pursue a remedy.

Please contact us at `copyright@packtpub.com` with a link to the suspected \pirated material.

We appreciate your help in protecting our authors, and our ability to bring you valuable content.

Questions

You can contact us at `questions@packtpub.com` if you are having a problem with any aspect of the book, and we will do our best to address it.

Building a Game Application 1

In this chapter we will set up our Visual Studio project and build a basic OpenGL application from scratch. We will be using this application throughout the book by extending its capabilities and introducing more features in the later chapters.

We are not going to build anything as complex as the latest multimillion dollar budget First-person shooter or Real-time strategy games in a scant 100 pages, but we are going to learn as much as we can about using OpenGL graphics and Bullet physics by writing small 3D demos. These demos will teach you the foundations necessary to build customized physics and graphical effects in other game projects. Sounds fun? Then let's get started!

Application components

In order to create the simple 3D game demo applications of this book, we will need the following four essential components:

- Application layer
- Physics
- Graphics
- Input handling

The reason for the application layer should be pretty obvious; it provides a starting point to work with, even if it's just a blank window. Meanwhile, we need the remaining components to provide two important elements of any game: visuals and interactivity. If you can't see anything, and you can't interact with it, it would be quite a stretch to claim that what you have is a game!

These are the essential building blocks or components of most games and game engines, and it's important to note that each of them is independent of the rest. When we write code to implement or change the visualization of our objects, we don't want to have to worry about changing anything in the physics system at the same time. This decoupling makes it easy to make these components as simple or complex as we desire.

Of course, a modern game or game engine will have many more components than this, such as networking, animation, resource management, and even audio; but these won't be necessary for the applications in this book since we are focussed on learning about physics and graphics with two specific libraries: Bullet and OpenGL respectively. However, the beauty of component-based design is that there's nothing that stops us from grabbing an audio library such as FMOD and giving the demos some much needed sound effects and background music, thus bringing them one step closer to being real games.

Bullet is a physics engine and it is important to realize that Bullet is only a physics simulation solution. It does not provide a means for visualizing its objects and it never promises to. The authors of the library assume that we will provide an independent means of rendering, so that they can focus on making the library as feature-rich in physics as possible. Therefore, in order to visualize Bullet's objects, we will be using OpenGL. But, OpenGL itself is a very low-level library that is as close to the graphics-card hardware as you can get. This makes it very unwieldy, complicated, and frustrating to work with, unless you really want to get into the nuts and bolts of 3D graphics.

To spare us from such hair-pulling frustration, we will be using **FreeGLUT**. This is a library which encapsulates and simplifies OpenGL instructions (such libraries are often called **wrappers**) and, as a bonus, takes care of application bootup, control, and input handling as well. So, with just Bullet and FreeGLUT, we have everything that we need to begin building our first game application.

Exploring the Bullet and FreeGLUT projects

Packaged versions of the Bullet and FreeGLUT projects can be found with this book's source code, which can be downloaded from the PACKT website at: `http://www.packtpub.com/learning-game-physics-with-bullet-physics-and-opengl/book`

Note that this book uses Bullet Version 2.81. As of the time of writing, Bullet is undergoing an overhaul in Version 3.x to make use of multiprocessor environments and push physics processing onto GPUs. Check this github repository for more information:

`http://github.com/erwincoumans/bullet3`

Bullet and FreeGLUT can also be downloaded from their respective project websites:

- `http://bulletphysics.org`
- `http://freeglut.sourceforge.net`

Bullet and FreeGLUT are both open source libraries, licensed under the `zlib` and `X-Consortium/MIT` licenses, respectively. The details can be found at:

`http://opensource.org/licenses/zlib-license.php`

`http://opensource.org/licenses/MIT`

Also, the main website for OpenGL itself is: `http://www.opengl.org`

Exploring Bullet's built-in demo applications

A lot of the designing and coding throughout this book is based upon, and very closely mimics the design of Bullet's own demo applications. This was intentional for good reason; if you can understand everything in this book, you can dig through all of Bullet's demo applications without having to absorb hundreds of lines of code at once. You will also have an understanding of how to use the API from top to bottom.

One significant difference between this book and Bullet's demos is that Bullet uses **GLUT (OpenGL Utility Toolkit)** for rendering, while this book uses **FreeGLUT**. This library was chosen partly because FreeGLUT is open source, allowing you to browse through its internals if you wish to, and partly because GLUT has not received an update since 1998 (the main reason why FreeGLUT was built to replace it). But, for our purposes, GLUT and FreeGLUT are essentially identical, even down to the function names they use, so it should be intuitive to compare and find similarities between Bullet's demo applications and the applications we will be building throughout this book.

You can examine the Bullet application demos by opening the following project file in Visual Studio:

```
<Bullet installation folder>\build\vs2010\0BulletSolution.sln
```

This would be a good time to open this project, compile, and launch some demos. This will help us to get a feel for the kinds of applications we will be building.

To run a different project, right-click on one of the projects, select **Set as StartUp Project**, and hit *F5*.

Starting a new project

Linking the library and header files into a new project can be an exhausting process, but it is essential for building a new standalone project. However, to keep things simple, the Chapter1.1_EmptyProject project in the book's source code has all of the headers and library files included with an empty main() function ready for future development. If you wish to examine how these projects are pieced together, take the time to explore their project properties in Visual Studio.

Here is a screenshot of the files extracted from the book's source code, and made ready for use:

Name	Date modified	Type	Size
Bullet	8/22/2013 6:34 PM	File folder	
Chapter1.1_EmptyProject	8/22/2013 6:34 PM	File folder	
FreeGLUT	8/22/2013 6:34 PM	File folder	
freeglut.dll	8/22/2013 6:32 PM	Application extens...	312 KB

Note that FreeGLUT also relies on freeglut.dll being placed in the project's working folder. Normally this requires the FreeGLUT project to be compiled first, but since it's packaged with the book's source code, this is unnecessary.

Building the application layer

Now we can begin to build an application layer. The purpose of this layer is to separate essential communication with the Windows operating system from our custom application logic. This allows our future demo applications to be more focused, and keep our codebase clean and re-usable.

 Continue from here using the Chapter1.2_TheApplicationLayer project files.

Configuring FreeGLUT

Handling low-level operating system commands, particularly for a graphical application, can be a tedious and painful task, but the FreeGLUT library was created to help people like us to create OpenGL-based applications and avoid such burdens. The trade-off is that when we launch our application, we effectively hand the majority of control over to the FreeGLUT library.

We can still control our application, but only through a series of callback functions. Each callback has a unique purpose, so that one might be used when its time to render the scene, and another is used when keyboard input is detected. This is a common design for utility toolkits such as FreeGLUT. We will be keeping all of our application layer code within a single class called BulletOpenGLApplication.

Downloading the example code

You can download the example code files for all Packt books you have purchased from your account at http://www.packtpub. com. If you purchased this book elsewhere, you can visit http:// www.packtpub.com/support and register to have the files e-mailed directly to you.

Here is a code snippet of the basic class declaration for BulletOpenGLApplication:

```
class BulletOpenGLApplication {
public:
  BulletOpenGLApplication();
  ~BulletOpenGLApplication();
  void Initialize();
  virtual void Keyboard(unsigned char key, int x, int y);
  virtual void KeyboardUp(unsigned char key, int x, int y);
  virtual void Special(int key, int x, int y);
```

```
   virtual void SpecialUp(int key, int x, int y);
   virtual void Reshape(int w, int h);
   virtual void Idle();
   virtual void Mouse(int button, int state, int x, int y);
   virtual void PassiveMotion(int x, int y);
   virtual void Motion(int x, int y);
   virtual void Display();
};
```

These essential functions make up the important hooks of our application layer class. The functions have been made virtual to enable us to extend or override them in future projects.

As mentioned previously, FreeGLUT has different functions for different purposes, such as when we press a key, or resize the application window. In order for FreeGLUT to know which function to call at what moment, we make a series of calls that map specific actions to a custom list of callback functions. Since these calls will only accept function pointers that follow specific criteria in return value and input parameters, we are restricted to using the arguments listed in the previous functions.

Meanwhile, by their nature, callback functions must call to a known, constant place in memory; hence a static function fits the bill. But, static functions cannot perform actions on nonstatic or nonlocal objects. So, we either have to turn the functions in BulletOpenGLApplication static, which would be incredibly ugly from a programming perspective, or we have to find a way to give it a local reference by passing it as a parameter. However, we just determined that the arguments have already been decided by FreeGLUT and we cannot change them.

The workaround for this is to store our application in a global static pointer during initialization.

```
static BulletOpenGLApplication* g_pApp;
```

With this pointer our callback functions can reach an instance of our application object to work with at any time. Meanwhile an example declaration of one of our callbacks is written as follows:

```
static void KeyboardCallback(unsigned char key, int x, int y);
```

The only purpose of each of these callback functions is to call the equivalent function in our application class through the global static pointer, as follows:

```
static void KeyboardCallback(unsigned char key, int x, int y) {
  g_pApp->Keyboard(key, x, y);
}
```

Next, we need to hook these functions into FreeGLUT. This can be accomplished using the following code:

```
glutKeyboardFunc(KeyboardCallback);
```

The previous command tells FreeGLUT to map our `KeyboardCallback()` function to any *key-down* events. The following section lists FreeGLUT functions which accomplish a similar task for other types of events.

glutKeyboardFunc/glutKeyboardUpFunc

The `glutKeyboardFunc` and `glutKeyboardUpFunc` functions are called when FreeGLUT detects that a keyboard key has been pressed down or up, respectively. These functions only work for keyboard characters that can be represented by a `char` data type (`glutSpecialFunc` and `glutSpecialUpFunc` handle other types).

Some applications and game engines may only call the input function once the key is pressed down, and only sends another signal when the key is released, but nothing in-between. Meanwhile, others may buffer the inputs allowing you to poll it at later times to check the current state of any key or input control, while others may provide a combination of both methods allowing you to choose which method works best for you.

By default, FreeGLUT calls this function repeatedly while a key is held down, but this behavior can be toggled globally with the `glutSetKeyRepeat()` and `glutIgnoreKeyRepeat()` commands.

glutSpecialFunc/glutSpecialUpFunc

The `glutSpecialFunc` and `glutSpecialUpFunc` functions are similar to the previous keyboard commands, but called for special keys such as *Home*, *Insert*, the arrow keys, and so on.

glutMouseFunc

The `glutMouseFunc` function is called when mouse button input is detected. This applies to both button up and button down events, which can be distinguished from the `state` parameter it sends.

glutMotionFunc/glutPassiveMotionFunc

The `glutMotionFunc` and `glutPassiveMotionFunc` functions are called when mouse movement is detected. The `glutMotionFunc()` function is used when any mouse button is currently held down, while the `glutPassiveMotionFunc()` function is used when no mouse buttons are pressed.

glutReshapeFunc

The `glutReshapeFunc` function is called when FreeGLUT detects that the application window has changed its shape. This is necessary for the graphics system (and sometimes game logic) to know the new screen size and it's up to us to make important changes to the scene to handle all possibilities.

glutDisplayFunc

If FreeGLUT determines that the current window needs to be redrawn, the `glutDisplayFunc` function is called. Sometimes Windows detects that an application window is in a damaged state, such as when another window has been partially obscuring it, and this is where this function might be called. We would typically just re-render the scene here.

glutIdleFunc

The `glutIdleFunc` function fills the role of the typical update of game applications. It is called when FreeGLUT is not busy processing its own events, giving us time to perform our own game logic instructions.

More information about these functions can be found in the FreeGLUT documentation at: `http://freeglut.sourceforge.net/docs/api.php`

Initializing FreeGLUT

Finally, we need to configure our application window before FreeGLUT can launch it for us. This is done through the following function calls:

```
glutInit(&argc, argv);
glutInitDisplayMode(GLUT_DOUBLE | GLUT_RGBA | GLUT_DEPTH);
glutInitWindowPosition(0, 0);
glutInitWindowSize(width, height);
glutCreateWindow(title);
glutSetOption (GLUT_ACTION_ON_WINDOW_CLOSE,
  GLUT_ACTION_GLUTMAINLOOP_RETURNS);
```

The following section provides a brief description of each of the previous function calls.

glutInit

The glutInit function performs first-step initialization of the FreeGLUT library, passing in the application's parameters. There are several low-level options one can play with here (such as enabling debugging in FreeGLUT itself), but we're not interested in them for our demos. Check the documentation for more information about the available options.

glutInitDisplayMode

The glutInitDisplayMode function sets the initial display mode of the window, mostly in terms of what kind of buffers are available. It uses a bitmask to set the values and the call shown previously enables a double-buffered window (GLUT_DOUBLE), make these buffers include an alpha channel (GLUT_RGBA), and also include a separate depth buffer (GLUT_DEPTH). We'll explain these concepts more throughout the book. There are many more options available, so those who are curious can check the online documentation.

> Note that RGBA is a short form for the three primary colors; red, green, and blue, and A is short form for alpha, or transparency. This is a common form of describing a single color value in computer graphics.

glutInitWindowPosition/glutInitWindowSize

The glutInitWindowPosition and glutInitWindowSize functions set the initial position and size of the window in pixels. The position is set relative to the top-left of the main screen.

glutCreateWindow

The glutCreateWindow function spawns a top-level window for the Windows OS to manage, and sets the title we want it to display in the title bar.

glutSetOption

The glutSetOption function is used to configure a number of options in the window, even the values that we've already edited such as the display mode and the window size. The two options passed in the previous example ensure that when the main window is closed, the main loop will return, exiting our game logic. The main loop itself will be explained in the following section.

Launching FreeGLUT

The final and possibly most important function in FreeGLUT is `glutMainloop()`. The moment this function is called, we hand the responsibility of application management over to the FreeGLUT library. From that point forward, we only have control when FreeGLUT calls the callback functions we mapped previously.

In our project code, all of the listed functions are encapsulated with a global function called `glutmain()`, which accepts an instance of our application class as a parameter, stores it in our global pointer, calls its own `Initialize()` function (because even our application class will want to know when the application is powering up), and then calls the `glutMainloop()` function.

And so, finally, we have everything in place to write the all-powerful `main()` function. In this chapter's source code, the `main()` function looks as follows:

```
int main(int argc, char** argv)
{
  BulletOpenGLApplication demo;
  return glutmain(argc, argv, 1024, 768, "Introduction to Game
Physics with Bullet Physics and OpenGL", &demo);
}
```

Before proceeding, try to compile and run the application from this chapter's source code (*F5* in Visual Studio). A new window should launch with either a plain-white or garbled background (depending on various low-level Windows configuration settings) as shown in the following screenshot. Do not worry if you see a garbled background for now as this will be resolved later.

It is also worth checking that the callback functions are working properly by adding breakpoints to them and verifying that they trigger each frame, and/or when you press a key or click on a mouse button.

Summary

Building a standalone project that hooks into other libraries is the first step towards building an application. We skipped most of this grunt work by using a prebuilt template; but if you're just starting out with the game development, it is important to understand and practice this process for the future, since this will not be the last time you have to tinker with Visual Studio project properties!

The most interesting lesson we learned is how to keep our application layer code in a separate class, and how to get hooks into the FreeGLUT library, thus giving it control over our application.

In the next chapter, we will introduce two of the most important parts of any game: graphics and user input!

2
Rendering and User Input

In this chapter, we will begin our journey into the world of OpenGL by performing some basic initialization steps, and rendering an object onto our window. Then we will learn how to gather user inputs, and how to manipulate the camera using that input in order to view our 3D scene from any angle.

Rendering the scene

In its most basic form, 3D rendering involves four essential tasks:

- Creating a blank canvas on which to draw
- Painting every object in the world onto the canvas, based on the direction it is being viewed from (by the camera)
- Copying the canvas image to the screen
- Clearing the canvas and repeating the process

However, there is much more nuance and complication involved in this process than it might first appear. In this section, we will explore some of the complications of 3D rendering and how they are typically worked around. In-depth explanations of these topics are beyond the scope of this book, and could fill entire chapters by themselves. But, we'll give each of them a cursory examination so that we're not left completely in the dark.

 Continue from here using the Chapter2.1_RenderingTheScene project files.

Introducing double-buffering

One complete cycle of the previous tasks is often called a single frame, and when the cycle is repeated multiple times per second, this gives us the frame rate, or how many frames per second are being drawn. As long as the cycle is repeated often enough, and there are gradual differences in the position of the camera and the world's objects, then our brain interprets this information as an animated scene — much like an animated cartoon on TV. Other common words to describe these cycles are refresh, iteration, or render-call.

When we perform these tasks, the graphics system spends most of its time handling the second task: drawing the world's objects onto the canvas. When an object is rendered the graphics system picks the corresponding pixel in the canvas and sets the color of the object there.

This canvas is typically referred to as a buffer. Whenever lots of unique values of a common data type are stored together (in this case a unique color value for each pixel), we usually refer to it as a buffer.

When the display system is ready to draw the next frame, it grabs the current buffer from the video memory (which could be in a dedicated GPU or elsewhere) and copies it for us to be seen on the screen. The buffer is then cleared and the process repeats.

But, what happens if the graphics card has not finished rendering all of the objects before the screen grabs the buffer? If the two processes are not synchronized, it would result in rendering of partial frames which would look very obvious to the human eye and ruin the illusion we're trying to create.

To solve this problem, we will use two buffers instead of one; this is called **double-buffering**. At any moment, one buffer is being displayed (known as the **frontbuffer**) while the other is being drawn to (known as the **backbuffer**). When we've finished drawing onto the backbuffer, we swap the buffers around so that the second is being displayed, while we draw onto the first. We repeat this process over and over again to ensure that we never draw onto the same buffer that we're displaying. This results in a more consistent scene without the graphical glitches.

Note that we have already enabled this feature back in *Chapter 1, Building a Game Application*, when we called the glutInitDisplayMode() function.

The following diagram shows the working of double-buffering:

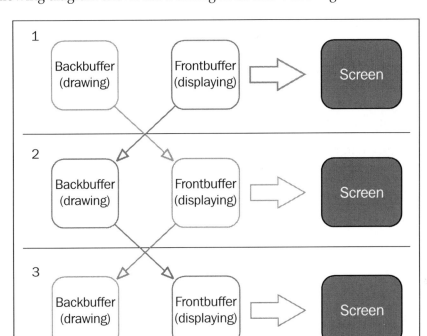

The command to swap these buffers in FreeGLUT is `glutSwapBuffers()`, and the command to clear the backbuffer is `glClear()`. In order to clear the color value of every pixel in the current buffer, we pass the value `GL_COLOR_BUFFER_BIT` into `glClear()`. Both of these functions must be called inside the `Idle()` function, which is automatically and repeatedly called by FreeGLUT whenever it's not busy processing its own events. This is the moment where we should process our own background tasks such as physics processing, object management, responding to game events, and even rendering itself.

In order to set the clearing color, we call the `glClearColor()` function as follows:

```
glClearColor(0.6, 0.65, 0.85, 0);
```

The given values should result in a light-blue color that is 60 percent red, 65 percent green, and 85 percent blue. The fourth parameter is the alpha (transparency) value, and is typically set to 0 in this situation. The following screenshot shows our application window, and now that glClear() is being called every iteration:

Understanding the basics of a camera

In order to visualize objects in our scene, a **camera** is required. The mathematics involved in camera control and movement can be quite confusing, so we'll explore it more in-depth towards the end of this chapter. For now, we will simply discuss a stationary camera.

An essential concept in 3D rendering is the transformation matrix, and the most important of which, that are used time and time again, are the **view** and **projection** matrices. The view matrix represents the camera's position/rotation in space, and where it's facing, while the projection matrix represents the camera's aspect ratio and bounds (also known as the camera's **frustum**), and how the scene is stretched/warped to give an appearance of depth (which we call perspective).

One of the most important properties of matrices is being able to combine two matrices together, through a simple matrix multiplication, and resulting in a transformation matrix that represents both. This property massively cuts down the amount of mathematics that needs to be performed every time we render the scene.

In OpenGL, we must select the matrix we wish to modify with `glMatrixMode()`. From that point onwards, or until `glMatrixMode()` is called again, any matrix-modifying commands will affect the selected matrix. We will be using this command to select the projection (`GL_PROJECTION`) and view (`GL_MODELVIEW`) matrices.

glIdentity

The `glIdentity` function sets the currently selected matrix to the **identity** matrix, which is effectively the matrix equivalent of the number one. The identity matrix is most often used to initialize a matrix to a default value before calling future functions described in the following sections.

glFrustum

The `glFrustum` function multiplies the currently selected matrix by a projection matrix defined by the parameters fed into it. This generates our perspective effect (mentioned previously), and when applied, creates the illusion of depth. It accepts six values describing the left, right, bottom, top, near, and far clipping planes of the camera's frustum: essentially the six sides of a 3D trapezoid (or trapezoidal prism in technical terms). The following diagram is an example of a camera frustum, where **FOV** stands for **field of view**:

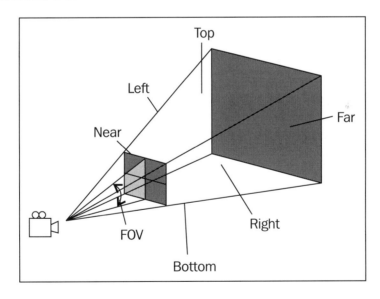

gluLookAt

The `gluLookAt` function multiplies the currently selected matrix by a view matrix generated from nine `doubles` (essentially three vectors), which represents the eye position, the point at which the camera is looking at, and a vector that represents which direction is up. The up vector is used to assist in defining the camera's rotation. To use common angular rotation vernacular, if we only define a position and target, that gives us the pitch and yaw we need, but there's still the question of the roll, so we use the up vector to help us calculate it.

glViewport

Finally, `glViewport()` is used to describe the current `Viewport`, or where we should draw the current camera's view of the scene in the application window. Typically, this would stretch to the bounds of the window from 0, 0 to w, h (where w and h are the screen width/height respectively), but this can be used to define whatever viewport is required.

The `glViewport()` function should be called each time when FreeGLUT calls the `Reshape()` function, which is called every time when the window size changes, passing us the new height and width. It's also called once when the application is first launched.

In order to maintain data for our camera, we will keep the following member variables in our application class so that we can refer to them as needed:

```
btVector3 m_cameraPosition;
btVector3 m_cameraTarget;
btVector3 m_upVector;
float m_nearPlane;
float m_farPlane;
```

 Throughout this book we will be using Bullet's built-in vector, quaternion, and matrix classes for our 3D mathematics to spare us from having to build our own from scratch.

Meanwhile, the code to update our camera is called within the `Idle()` function. The comments in the chapter's source code will explain the details of this function. If any of the commands in the `UpdateCamera()` function don't make much sense, then go back to the start of this section and refamiliarize yourself with the purpose of the various `gl-` commands, when the FreeGLUT callback functions are triggered, and how they are used.

Basic rendering and lighting

We will now construct a simple object from the primitive shapes (triangles), and explore how OpenGL's built-in lighting system can help us to visualize our object in three dimensions.

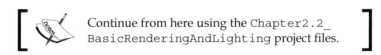

Continue from here using the `Chapter2.2_BasicRenderingAndLighting` project files.

Creating a simple box

The `glBegin()` and `glEnd()` functions are the two important OpenGL commands that work together to define the starting and ending points (known as **delimiters**) for the construction of a primitive shape. The `glBegin()` function requires a single argument that specifies the type of primitive to render. This determines whether the vertices we input represent points, lines, triangles, quads, or whatever the renderer supports. We'll be using `GL_TRIANGLES` for our box, each of which requires three unique vertices in space in order to render.

There are a variety of commands that can be called between `glBegin()` and `glEnd()` to build the primitive, but the two commands that we will be using are `glVertex3f()`, which defines the position of a vertex in space, and `glColor3f()` which sets the color of subsequent vertices using the same RGB system that we saw in the previous chapter (note that it does not have an alpha value).

The actual task of rendering the box happens in the `DrawBox()` function of the chapter's source code. The most important part is as follows:

```
static int indices[36] = {
  0,1,2, 3,2,1, 4,0,6, 6,0,2, 5,1,4, 4,1,0, 7,3,1, 7,1,5, 5,4,7,
  7,4,6, 7,2,3, 7,6,2};
glBegin (GL_TRIANGLES);
for (int i = 0; i < 36; i += 3) {
  const btVector3 &vert1 = vertices[indices[i]];
  const btVector3 &vert2 = vertices[indices[i+1]];
  const btVector3 &vert3 = vertices[indices[i+2]];
  glVertex3f (vert1.x(), vert1.y(), vert1.z());
  glVertex3f (vert2.x(), vert2.y(), vert2.z());
  glVertex3f (vert3.x(), vert3.y(), vert3.z());
}
glEnd();
```

`DrawBox()` creates a closed box object based on the size of the dimensions we wish to build it from. The input parameter is `btVector3`, providing the three dimensions of the box. `DrawBox()` then uses the concept of indices to iterate through the number of vertices we want, without having to repeat the data. We could create the box from 36 different points, but really there are only eight unique points on a box. Indexes work by labelling each of these eight points with a unique number (index) from 0 to 7, and use those to define the triangles, instead. Here is a screenshot of our box with no lighting applied:

Let there be light!

At this stage, we can see our box, but all of its faces have exactly the same coloring, which makes it a little difficult to determine the exact shape as it moves around in space. OpenGL has some basic built-in lighting functionality, which we will make use of.

Normals

Normals represent the direction pointing away from a given surface or point. They are used in a variety of useful techniques (and not just lighting!), and the most basic of which is simple diffuse lighting or lighting an object based on the angle between the light source and the surface. Our lighting system will use each point's normal to decide in which direction the incoming light should reflect away from that surface helping it calculate the overall color of the polygon.

Setting the normal for a given vertex can be accomplished by calling the `glNormal3f()` function. This function sets the normal for the subsequent vertices, which could be more than one in the case where they all share the same normal value until `glNormal3f()` is called again. For the record, `glColor3f()` functions in the same way. The renderer assumes that you're using the same color and normal for each new vertex until you specify otherwise.

The normal can be calculated fairly easily by performing a cross-product on the three vertices that make up the triangle. If we remember our 3D mathematics, this gives us a vector perpendicular to the vectors of all three vertices. The cross product is noncommutative, so the output vector could either point inwards or outwards from the surface, depending on what order we performed the cross product, but fixing it is simply a matter of multiplying it by -1.

Creating ambient, diffuse, and specular lighting

There are three basic lighting effects that were some of the earliest lighting effects produced in 3D graphics and are still used to today to simulate basic and cheap lighting effects in a 3D environment.

Ambient lighting is used to simulate the base background lighting of a scene. It is essentially the minimum color value of every pixel in the scene in the absence of any other light sources; so if we had an ambient lighting value of (0.3,0.3,0.3), and there were no other light sources present, everything we render would be colored dark grey. Computationally, this effect is cheap.

Diffuse lighting, as mentioned earlier, depends on the direction of the light and simulates the effect of light radiating from a source and rebounding off the surfaces. The shallower the angle between the direction of the light and the surface, the weaker the effect that the light will have on that surface. This effect requires additional mathematics compared to ambient lighting (essentially one dot-product per vertex per light) to determine the output.

Finally, **specular** lighting represents the shininess of an object by highlighting certain areas with a brighter color depending on the angle of the camera with the light source. Because the camera also gets involved, the effect itself changes as the camera moves, and requires a greater amount of mathematics to produce.

However, despite of the difference in mathematical requirements, these three effects are almost trivialized by modern GPUs, and there are far more advanced and realistic visual effects such as global illumination, refraction, depth of field, HDR lighting, and so on, making these simple lighting effects a drop in the ocean by comparison.

The following diagram shows the same object rendered with ambient, ambient plus diffuse, and ambient plus diffuse plus specular lighting, respectively.

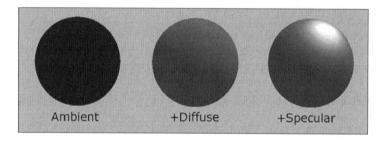

Understanding depth testing

Depth testing is an important part of graphical rendering that specifies how objects should be redrawn over others. To draw a painting in the real world, we must layer our objects on top of others in the correct order, as we start with the sky, then we add a hill on top of the sky, and then add a tree on top of the hill. But, if we draw our tree first, then overdraw with the hill, and then overdraw again with the sky, we would be left with just the sky on our canvas, and an incorrect representation of what we wanted.

The following diagram shows three objects rendered with and without depth testing enabled, respectively. The order of rendering is the small box, the large box, and then the sphere. The small box is closer to the camera, but without depth testing, the small box will be overdrawn by the remaining two. When depth testing is enabled, the renderer understands not to overdraw an object that is closer to the camera.

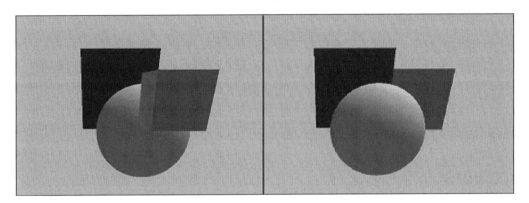

We need to store this depth information each time we render a new object so we know the depth of the object currently drawn there; but we can't use the original backbuffer to store this information since, there's just not enough information stored in a single RGBA value to do so. So, to keep a track of this information, we add another buffer called the **depth buffer**. Each time we attempt to render a pixel, we check the depth value of the pixel from the depth buffer (also known as the **z-buffer**, because it keeps track of the z-value of each pixel away from the camera). If the pixel is closer, then we render the object's color pixel to the backbuffer, and write the new z-value into the depth buffer. The next time we try to render at that pixel location, we will have the updated value to compare with.

 Earlier in this chapter, we mentioned how we can set multiple flags in `glClear()`, to clear certain buffers. The `GL_DEPTH_BUFFER_BIT` flag is used to clear the depth buffer each render call.

Let's go over some of the important OpenGL functions used for a basic lighting and depth testing system. In each case, there are more options available in the OpenGL documentation, which can be examined at your leisure.

glLightfv

The `glLightfv()` function is used to specify the properties of a given light. The first parameter is used to select which light to edit, the second is used to determine which property to edit, and the third is used to specify the new value. The first two parameters must be an enumerator (or enum) corresponding to a specific value. For instance, the options for the first parameter can be `GL_LIGHT0`, `GL_LIGHT1`, `GL_LIGHT2`, and so on. Meanwhile, the second parameter could be `GL_AMBIENT`, `GL_DIFFUSE`, or `GL_SPECULAR` to define which lighting property of the given light to modify, or even `GL_POSITION` to define its position. As an example, the following call sets the ambient lighting value of the first (zeroth) light to the value of `ambient`, where `ambient` is `btVector3` representing the ambient color we want:

```
glLightfv(GL_LIGHT0, GL_AMBIENT, ambient);
```

glEnable

The `glEnable()` function is a very generic function used to enable certain features in the OpenGL library. Every feature we enable typically consumes more processing power, so OpenGL gives us the freedom to enable only what we need. We will use this function to enable lighting in general (`GL_LIGHTING`), create a single light (`GL_LIGHT0`), enable the coloring of our primitives (`GL_COLOR_MATERIAL`), and enable depth testing (`GL_DEPTH_TEST`).

glMaterialfv/glMateriali

The `glMaterialfv` and `glMateriali` functions specify material parameters for the lighting system. Specifically, we will be using them to define the strength of our specular lighting effect. The first parameter for both functions can either be `GL_FRONT`, `GL_BACK`, or both combined to define if the setting should affect front or back faces (faces pointing towards or away from the camera — which is determined by using the normal).

We will be using them as follows:

```
glMaterialfv(GL_FRONT, GL_SPECULAR, specular);
glMateriali(GL_FRONT, GL_SHININESS, 15);
```

The first call sets the color of the specular effect through `GL_SPECULAR` (we re-use the specular variable for convenience since it already defines a white color). The second sets the shininess (`GL_SHININESS`) to a value of `15`. Larger values produce weaker shine effects, and vice versa.

glShadeModel

The glShadeModel() function sets the current style of lighting to either GL_FLAT or GL_SMOOTH. This is most noticeable on objects such as spheres. Flat shading is less computationally expensive, but provides a less believable lighting model. Even though the performance hit is barely noticeable on modern GPUs, it can be used for a particular artistic style, as shown in the following screenshot:

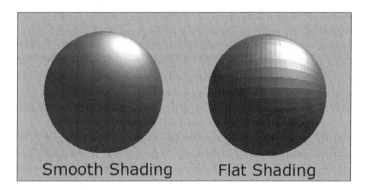

This effect is achieved by using the previously mentioned normals. With a flat shading model, the face is colored based on the direction of the light and the normal of the first vertex on the face, and it assumes that the normal value for the rest is the same. Hence, the mathematics used to calculate the diffuse lighting color of each pixel on the face will result in the exact same color. Smooth shading, on the other hand, calculates a separate result for each vertex independently, and then blends the computed color for each pixel between them. It is a very primitive lighting effect, but gives our objects a more believable appearance.

glDepthFunc

The glDepthFunc function sets the depth testing function the renderer will use, which could be one of the following options:

- GL_ALWAYS
- GL_NEVER
- GL_GREATER
- GL_LESS

These options specify whether the pixel should be overwritten with new information in one of four ways: always, never, if the z-value is greater than the current value (further away), or less than the current value (closer). The most common approach is to choose GL_LESS, but never let it to be said that OpenGL didn't give us the power to create whatever weird and wacky graphical effects we want, since choosing the other values will result in some interesting scenes (just use your imagination and the tree/hill/sky example from earlier).

So with this knowledge, inside the Initialize() function, we create a light at position (5,10,1) with ambient, diffuse, and specular properties, set the shading model to smooth lighting (GL_SMOOTH), and set the depth testing function to only overwrite pixels if their depth value is less than the existing value (GL_LESS). And voila! We have lighting enabled in our scene. Here is our box with basic lighting applied:

Coloring your box

If you recall, we called glColor3f() in our DrawBox() function, and set the default color parameter in the function's declaration to an RGB value of (1,1,1). This represents the white color: 100 percent red, green, and blue in additive coloring. Since we're not passing a value for this parameter in our DrawBox() call, it is still defaulting to white. Therefore, in order to change the color of our box, we simply add a color value to our DrawBox() call in the form of a btVector3.

```
DrawBox(btVector3(1, 1, 1), btVector3(1.0f, 0.2f, 0.2f));
```

Feel free to tweak the highlighted values until you find a color you prefer.

 Note that even though color itself is not a vector, a `btVector3` is a convenient object to use to store three unique floats.

Understanding rendering pipelines

So far (and throughout the remainder of this book), we have performed rendering through a technique called **immediate mode**, where the graphics system essentially forgets the information of each render-call, and must be reminded of the data every time we draw. We have witnessed this in our `DrawBox()` function, where we literally rewrite the information to define and draw our box every single time the function is called, and it is called every single render-call. This is obviously not the most efficient way of doing things!

Immediate mode is opposite to **retained mode** where vertex data is stored (retained) within memory, and recalled by the graphics system when requested. The retained mode method consumes more memory during runtime, but it is much faster and more efficient. However, it can be difficult to understand and use when you're just starting with the 3D graphics.

In addition, there are two types of high-level rendering process called the **fixed-function pipeline** and the **programmable pipeline**. All of the code in this book performs its rendering using the fixed-function pipeline. It is called so because it follows a fixed series of function calls to draw the graphical elements to the screen, such as processing the primitives, performing transforms and lighting, coloring, depth testing, and so on. The important point to make here is that the order of these steps cannot be changed and you have a limited amount of control over each step.

The more modern form of rendering is the programmable pipeline. It is much more fluid, allowing the graphics programmer to have an immense amount of control over the rendering steps through the use of custom scripts called **shaders**. Shaders can vary from very simple scripts that render objects with ambient shading, to complex procedures that render effects such as motion blur, HDR lighting, produce millions of pixel-sized particles, depth of field, and many more. There are even several languages that can be used to write shaders (common ones are Cg, GLSL, and HLSL), and they can be used to produce any graphical effect you want to render (depending on performance limitations, of course). Entire volumes can, and have been written on the nuances of writing shaders with all the various languages, algorithms, and styles of programming they support, making their understanding a highly skilled and highly valued area of 3D graphics programming.

But, don't feel that you've wasted time learning the fixed-function pipeline, because the programmable pipeline can be utterly bewildering if you haven't established a firm grasp of the fundamentals through the fixed-function pipeline first.

User input and camera control

We will now learn how to gather keyboard input from FreeGLUT and use it to interact with our world. This will take the form of rotating our camera around the center of our world (and hence, our box).

 Continue from here using the `Chapter2.3_ UserInputAndCameraControl` project files.

Implementing camera control

We created a basic camera earlier in this chapter, but it is currently stationary. In order to verify that our world is truly three-dimensional, it would help if we could rotate our camera around a central pivot point. There's a lot of 3D mathematics that goes into controlling camera movement (particularly when it comes to rotation), which is beyond the scope of this book. So, if some of what is covered here seems confusing, know that pretty much any book or blog that covers 3D mathematics and rendering as a whole should cover these topics.

To begin, we will need three new variables for our camera. These will store the current values for the camera's rotation and zoom:

```
float m_cameraDistance; // distance from the camera to its target
float m_cameraPitch; // pitch of the camera
float m_cameraYaw; // yaw of the camera
```

Significant changes are required in our `UpdateCamera()` code to calculate the new camera position based on the previous variables. The additions to this function are liberally commented to explain the process, so we won't consume space explaining them here.

With our camera control code in place, we can manipulate its position by simply modifying the three new variables and calling `UpdateCamera()` to perform the required math for us. However, this isn't useful without some way of gathering input and making the necessary changes to the aforementioned variables.

Gathering user input

FreeGLUT allows us to gather input using the `Keyboard()` and `Special()` callback functions. Remember that `Keyboard()` is called whenever FreeGLUT detects that a generic keyboard key has been pressed, such as letters, numbers, and so on. Meanwhile, the `Special()` function is called for special keys such as the arrow keys, *Home*, *End*, *Page Up/Page Down*, and so on.

In this chapter's source code, we've used both of these functions to grab different types of user input, and employed them to modify our camera's pitch, yaw, and zoom distance (recall that the roll is always calculated using an up vector that never changes). Each time the values are modified by a key press, we perform the mathematical calculations necessary to reposition the camera based on this updated information. Note that these functions are repeatedly called while a key is still held down, allowing the camera to continue moving as long as the key is pressed.

Within our application, we can now zoom and rotate the camera with the arrow keys, *Z*, and *X*. Here is our box viewed from a different angle and distance:

Summary

We have delved into some OpenGL code and taken a crash course in 3D rendering, by exploring the basics of double-buffering, and camera initialization through the important view and projection matrices. We've used this knowledge to build a basic scene using primitive shapes, vertices, normals, depth testing, lighting, shading types, and finally, color. As confusing as they might seem, they all contribute to the building blocks from which all modern graphical techniques are born.

Finally, we created a simple and colored box, complete with a moveable camera and basic lighting effects. This will be our essential OpenGL application template going forward, and hopefully we learned a lot about the fundamentals of 3D graphics, OpenGL, and FreeGLUT from building it.

In the next chapter, we will begin to integrate our physics engine by creating and initializing Bullet's core components, and turn our cube into a rigid body which will fall under the effects of gravity!

3

Physics Initialization

In this chapter, we will discover how to initialize the Bullet library, and learn how to build our first physical rigid body object, which is the simplest object available in Bullet.

The core bullet objects

Bullet is designed from the ground up to be highly customizable. Each major task that the physics engine performs is isolated into its own modular component, allowing them to be replaced with ease as long as they inherit from the appropriate interface/base classes.

Most applications, such as ours, can make do with a generic, one-size-fits-all selection of components, but if we ever find ourselves needing something more advanced, optimized, or technically superior, then there is nothing stopping us from interchanging the components or even building our own.

There are a handful of components that need to be created and hooked together in order to initialize Bullet. We'll cover some essential theory on each of these components, and then run through the code to create/destroy them.

 Continue from here using the `Chapter3.1_TheCoreBulletObjects` project files.

The world object

The primary control object for a Bullet physics simulation is an instance of btDynamicsWorld. All of our physical objects will be controlled by the rules defined by this class. There are several types of btDynamicsWorld that can be used, depending on how you want to customize your physics simulation, but the one we will be using is btDiscreteDynamicsWorld. This world moves objects in discrete steps (hence the name) in space as time advances.

 This class doesn't define how to detect collisions, or how objects respond to collisions. It only defines how they move in response to stepping the simulation through time.

The broad phase

A physics simulation runs in real time, but it does so in discrete steps of time. Each step, there would be some number of objects which may have moved a small distance based on their motion and how much time has passed. After this movement has completed, a verification process checks whether a collision has occurred, and if so, then it must generate the appropriate response.

Generating an accurate collision response alone can be highly computationally expensive, but we also have to worry about how much time we spend checking for collisions in the first place. The brute force method is to make sure that no collisions have been missed by comparing every object against every other object, and finding any overlaps in space, and doing this *every* step.

This would be all well and good for simple simulations with few objects, but not when we potentially have hundreds of objects moving simultaneously, such as in a videogame. If we brute force our way through the collision checks, then we need to check all the N objects against the other N-1 objects. In Big O notation this is an $O(N^2)$ situation. This design scales badly for increasing values of N, generating an enormous performance bottleneck as the CPU buckles under the strain of having so much work to do every step. For example, if we have 100 objects in our world, then we have 100*99 = 9,900 pairs of objects to check!

Brute forcing one's way through physics collision detection is typically the first performance bottleneck an inexperienced game programmer comes across. Understanding what's happening, and how to optimize these kinds of bulk processes is a key component in becoming an effective game developer.

But, imagine if only two of those 100 objects are even remotely close together and the rest are spread too far apart to matter; why would we waste the time doing precise collision checks on the other 9,899 pairs? This is the purpose of **broad phase collision detection**. It is the process of quickly culling away object pairs, which have little or no chance of collision in the current step, and then creating a shortlist of those that could collide. This is an important point because the process merely provides a rough estimate, in order to keep the mathematics computationally cheap. It does not miss any legitimate collision pairs, but it will return some that aren't actually colliding.

Once we have shortlisted the potential collisions, we pass them on to another component of the physics simulation called narrow phase collision detection, which checks the shortlist for legitimate collisions using more intense, but accurate mathematical techniques.

For our project we will use a broad phase technique based on dynamic bounding volumes. This algorithm create volumes of space which envelop pairs of objects in a tree hierarchy using **Axis-aligned bounding boxes (AABBs)**. These AABBs surround the object with the smallest box shaped volume possible, that is aligned with each axis, as we can see here:

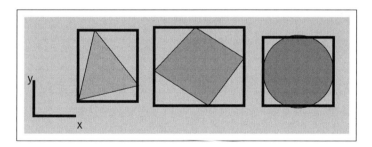

It is a relatively cheap task to check if two AABBs overlap, but we can still overburden ourselves if we don't perform some additional optimization. By organizing the objects by pairs in a tree structure, we naturally organize our objects by distance from one another, thus automatically culling away the object pairs which are too far apart to be worth checking, as we can see here:

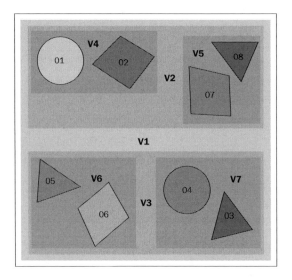

It takes some processing work to maintain the tree hierarchy as objects move around, since the AABBs have to be dynamically altered on occasion. But, this is much less expensive than performing AABB overlap checks on every pair, every iteration. You may recognize this tree structure as a simple binary tree:

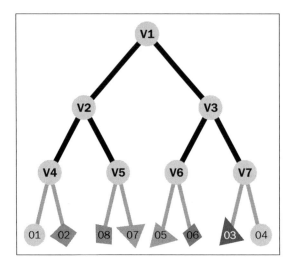

This is no coincidence. The intent is to use the simplicity and speed of searching a binary tree in order to quickly asses which objects are closest to others.

A `btBroadPhaseInterface` object is needed to tell our world object what technique to use for its broad phase collision detection and the built-in type we will be using is `btDbvtBroadphase`.

The collision configuration

This is a relatively simple component on the surface, but under the hood it provides the physics simulation with components that handle essential tasks such as determining how Bullet manages memory allocation, provides the algorithms for solving various collisions (box-box, sphere-box, and so on), and how to manage the data that comes out of the broad phase collision detection called **Manifolds** (we will explore these in *Chapter 6, Events, Triggers, and Explosions*).

For this project, we'll keep things simple and use Bullet's default collision configuration object, `btDefaultCollisionConfiguration`.

The collision dispatcher

The **collision dispatcher**, as the name implies, dispatches collisions into our application. For a video game, it is practically guaranteed that we will want to be informed of inter-object collision at some point, and this is the purpose of the collision dispatcher.

One of the built-in collision dispatcher class definitions that come with Bullet is the basic `btCollisionDispatcher`. The only requirement is that it must be fed with the collision configuration object in its constructor (which forces us to create this object second).

The constraint solver

The constraint solver's job is to make our objects respond to specific constraints. We will learn more about the constraints in *Chapter 5, Raycasting and Constraints*. We will be using `btSequentialImpulseConstraintSolver` for our project.

 Note that our application class will be derived from and customized in the `BasicDemo` class for the next several chapters. This keeps our application layer code isolated from our physics/game logic.

Each of the components described previously can be customized to fit our needs; for instance, we might be working within extremely tight memory requirements (such as a mobile device), and so we might consider completely replacing the stack allocator with our own to optimize Bullet's memory allocation processes.

Creating the Bullet components

Contrary to what the laborious explanations in the previous section might have you believe, creating the necessary Bullet objects is relatively simple. Our application layer class contains a handful of pointers that all the derived classes can use:

```
btBroadphaseInterface* m_pBroadphase;
btCollisionConfiguration* m_pCollisionConfiguration;
btCollisionDispatcher* m_pDispatcher;
btConstraintSolver* m_pSolver;
btDynamicsWorld* m_pWorld;
```

Meanwhile, the code to initialize Bullet can be found in `BasicDemo` and looks as shown in the following code snippet:

```
m_pCollisionConfiguration = new btDefaultCollisionConfiguration();
m_pDispatcher = new
  btCollisionDispatcher(m_pCollisionConfiguration);
m_pBroadphase = new btDbvtBroadphase();
m_pSolver = new btSequentialImpulseConstraintSolver();
m_pWorld = new btDiscreteDynamicsWorld(m_pDispatcher,
  m_pBroadphase, m_pSolver, m_pCollisionConfiguration);
```

Creating our first physics object

Bullet maintains the same modular design of its core components even down to individual physics objects. This allows us to customize physics objects through their components by interchanging or replacing them at will.

Three components are necessary to build a physics object in Bullet:

- A **collision shape**, defining the object's volume and how it should respond to the collisions with other collision shapes
- A **motion state**, which keeps track of the motion of the object
- A **collision object**, which acts as a master controller of the object, managing the previously mentioned components and the physical properties of the object

We'll cover some essential theory on these components before we build one in code. We'll also make some changes to our rendering system so that we can observe the effects of gravity on our object.

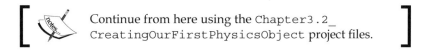

Continue from here using the `Chapter3.2_CreatingOurFirstPhysicsObject` project files.

The collision shape

The collision shape represents the volume of an object in space, be it a box, a sphere, a cylinder, or some other more complex shape. Collision shapes do not care about the rules of the world. They only care about how they should interact with other shapes, and so it is the collision shape's responsibility to inform Bullet what kind of shape it is, so that it can respond appropriately.

We will cover more varieties and intricacies of collision shapes in *Chapter 7, Collision Shapes*, but for now we will build a simple collision shape component using `btBoxShape`. This object's only requirement is to define its size upon creation.

As an interesting side note, spheres take a lot of polygons in order to generate an accurate graphical representation of them. But, the physical representation of a sphere is little more than a position and a radius, and calculating a sphere-to-sphere collision is very simple (check the distance between their centers against the sum of their radii). Meanwhile, a box is the exact opposite; they're cheap to generate graphically (only 12 triangles), but expensive to generate physically and requires much more complex mathematics to resolve collisions between them. Because of this, spheres are commonly used for the collision shape of an object, even if its graphical representation is not a sphere.

In addition, a newbie physics programmer would typically start out by using spheres to represent the bounding volumes for objects to generate their very first broad phase system. But, they will later graduate to using AABBs (similar to those described previously) as they find that the spheres are not very good at representing long, thin objects, and the mathematics aren't quite as efficient as AABB overlap checks. Even though AABBs are technically boxes, they don't rotate (since the AA stands for Axis-aligned), making the overlap math very simple—even simpler than comparing two spheres for overlap.

The motion state

The motion state's job is to catalogue the object's current position and orientation. This lets us to use it as a hook to grab the object's transformation matrix (also known as a transform). We can then pass the object's transform into our rendering system in order to update the graphical object to match that of the physics system.

This is an incredibly important point that cannot be ignored, forgotten, or otherwise misplaced; Bullet does not know, nor does it care, how we render its objects. We could add 100 physics objects into our application right now, and Bullet would move them, detect collisions, and resolve them as we would expect a physics engine to do; but unless we tell our OpenGL code to draw a graphical box object in the same location, we will have no idea about what's going on (besides doing some step through debugging and scanning the code, of course). Our physics and graphics engines are completely isolated from one another, and they have different ways of representing the same object.

Having no dependency between our graphics and physics is ideal because it means that we could completely replace the physics engine without having to touch the graphics engine, and vice versa. It also means that we can have invisible physics objects (such as force fields), or graphical objects that don't need a physical presence (such as particle effects).

It is not uncommon for a game engine to separate these components entirely with three different libraries, resulting in the three different sets of `Vector3`/`Matrix4x4`/`Quaternion` classes in the lowest levels; one set for the physics, one set for the graphics, and one set for general game logic.

As an example of extending Bullet, we will be creating our own motion state class called `OpenGLMotionState`. This class will extend Bullet's `btDefaultMotionState` to provide a useful helper function that simplifies the process of extracting the objects transform data into a format our rendering system can use.

The collision object

Collision objects are the essential building blocks of our physics objects, since they maintain the object's physical properties, and give us a hook from which to alter the object's velocity, acceleration, apply a force upon it, and so on. When we query the motion state for the transform, it actually comes to this object to obtain it.

The simplest and most commonly used type of collision object is a btRigidBody. Rigid bodies are physics objects that do not deform as a result of collisions, as opposed to soft bodies which do. Rigid bodies are the easiest collision objects to deal with because their behavior is consistent, and doesn't require extravagant mathematics to handle basic collisions, unlike soft bodies which are far more difficult and expensive to simulate.

Rigid bodies also require a btRigidBodyConstructionInfo object to be passed through their constructor. This object stores data of important physical properties for the rigid body, such as mass, friction, restitution, and so on.

Building a custom motion state

The entire code for our custom motion state can be found in a single header file OpenGLMotionState.h. The only interesting function is GetWorldTransform(), which takes an array of btScalars (16 of them to be precise, representing a 4 x 4 matrix), and performs a little math to return the same data in a format that OpenGL understands. getOpenGLMatrix() is a helper function built into btTransform that does this for us. OpenGL and Bullet are used together so often (*the* open source graphics library used together with *the* open source physics engine; who would have guessed?) that the developers of Bullet felt it was prudent to do this.

 btScalar is a simple float by default, but could also be a double if #define BT_USE_DOUBLE_PRECISION is placed somewhere in the code. We'll continue to use floats for this project.

It is a clean and efficient process to feed data between Bullet and OpenGL because they both use right-handed coordinate systems, which defines how the **x**, **y**, and **z** axes relate to one another. If we used a different physics and/or graphics library, we might find that our objects move or render backwards on one of the axes. In that case we may have a disconnection between our coordinate systems, and we would need to determine which axis has been flipped, and make the necessary adjustments. The following diagram shows the difference between the left-handed and right-handed coordinate systems:

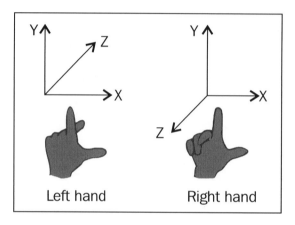

Creating a box

Creating a box-shaped rigid body is fairly simple; all of the code to create one can be found in the `CreateObjects()` function of this chapter's source code. We simply create the three modular components described previously (motion state, collision shape, and collision object), hook them together, and then inform the world object of its existence through `addRigidBody()`. The only awkward step is of using `btRigidBodyConstructionInfo`. This object is an intermediate step in creating `btRigidBody` and requires the mass, motion state, and collision shape objects before it can be built, although it has other properties that can be modified such as the coefficients of restitution (how much it bounces), and friction.

```
btRigidBody::btRigidBodyConstructionInfo rbInfo(1.0f,
    m_pMotionState, pBoxShape);
btRigidBody* pRigidBody = new btRigidBody(rbInfo);
```

Rendering from transform data

We still have the problem that our `DrawBox()` function always draws a box at (0,0,0) in world space. Before we can make use of the data from our object's motion state, we will have to modify our rendering system to draw our object at a given location instead. In order to do this, we'll need to introduce a few more OpenGL commands.

`glPushMatrix()` and `glPopMatrix()` are another pair of OpenGL delimiter functions that work together in much the same way as `glBegin()` and `glEnd()` do. They are used to control the **matrix stack**, which is very helpful while drawing multiple objects, and objects that are meant to be connected together. As mentioned previously, transformation matrices can be combined to get a resultant transformation, and if we have multiple objects that share a similar transformation, we can optimize our processing time by sharing information through the matrix stack, instead of recalculating the same value over and over again.

This feature is particularly useful when we have object hierarchies such as a knight riding on top of a steed, or moons orbiting planets, which themselves orbit stars. This is the basic concept of a Scene Graph in 3D rendering (which is beyond the scope of this book). The function to multiply the current matrix stack by a given matrix is `glMultMatrixf()`.

In this project, `DrawBox()` has been changed to collect an array of `btScalars` for the transform, and uses the methods explained previously to manipulate the matrix stack by surrounding the previous rendering code with calls to push and pop the stack.

 Note that the `/*REM*/` comment tags in the source code represent code that has been removed and/or replaced since the previous section.

Stepping the simulation

So, now we're rendering a graphical box in the same place as our physical box, but we still don't see it moving. This is because the box isn't actually moving. Why? Because Bullet has not been told to step the simulation, yet!

In order to do this, we simply call `stepSimulation()` on our `btDynamicsWorld` object, providing the number of seconds that have elapsed since the last iteration. The challenge here is counting the amount of time that has passed, since the last time we called `stepSimulation()`.

Bullet comes with a built-in btClock object, but if you have your own clock tool in mind, which you trust to be more precise, then there's nothing stopping you from using that for a counter instead. A good place to handle this logic is in the application layer class with the following member variable:

```
btClock m_clock;
```

The clock can be used to calculate the time since the last step and updating the application.

```
float dt = m_clock.getTimeMilliseconds();
m_clock.reset();
UpdateScene(dt / 1000.0f);
```

When we launch our application again, we should observe our box falling under the effects of gravity as in the following screenshot:

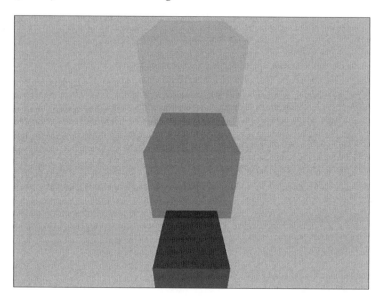

The stepSimulation() function also accepts two more parameters; the second parameter is the maximum number of substeps that can be calculated this iteration, and the third is the desired frequency of step calculations.

If we ask Bullet to perform calculations at a rate of 60 Hz (the third parameter – 60 Hz is also the default), but one second has gone by (maybe our application froze for a moment), Bullet will make 60 separate step calculations before returning. This prevents Bullet from jumping every object for one full second in time all at once, and possibly missing some collisions.

However, calculating so many iterations at once could take a long time to process, causing our simulation to slow down for a while as it tries to catch up. To solve this, we can use the second parameter to limit the maximum number of steps it's allowed to take in case one of these spikes occur. In this case, the world's physics will appear to slow down, but it also means that your application won't suffer from a long period of low frame rates.

In addition, the function returns the number of actual steps that took place, which will either be the maximum, or less if it processed everything quickly enough.

Summary

We've created the essential components that Bullet needs to initialize, and hooked them all together. We then created our first object in Bullet and extended our rendering system to render the object as it moves through space. To do this we created a custom class, OpenGLMotionState, which extends one of Bullet's own objects. This class simplifies the process of obtaining the correct OpenGL transform matrix from our object.

In the next chapter, we will implement a more robust system to handle multiple objects, and look into extracting useful physics debug information from Bullet.

4
Object Management and Debug Rendering

Our current application is not very scalable, and does not provide much in the way of debug information to help us work with the physics system. So in this chapter, we will be performing some code refactoring to help us handle these situations in a robust fashion.

Handling multiple objects

We're currently hard coding one pointer and making one call to `DrawBox()` to create our first object. Continuing down this path by adding a second pointer, and a second call to `DrawBox()` would make introducing even more objects into the scene an awkward and painful process.

A wise course of action to take at this early stage is to build a system that allows us to encapsulate important object data (such as the object's shape, collision shape, motion state, and color) in its own class. This way we can iterate through all of our objects, regardless of private information, and use common calls to update and render them.

In order to accomplish this, we will have to make five significant changes to our object system:

- Create a `GameObject` class to store our object's data
- Instantiate our objects from `GameObject` and store them in a data structure
- Modify our rendering system to iterate through the aforementioned data structure

- Have the rendering system detect the type of shape and render the appropriate polygons
- Write a new function to simplify the creation of objects

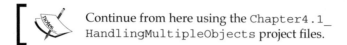

Continue from here using the `Chapter4.1_HandlingMultipleObjects` project files.

Designing our objects

We would like to create simple objects of various shapes such as boxes, spheres, and cylinders, and do so without having to repeat tasks such as creating the motion state, the rigid body, the rigid body construction info, and so on. Essentially, the only data that should be unique between any two objects are:

- The mass
- The shape
- The color
- The initial position and rotation

Because of this, it should be possible to create new objects using only these four parameters, while we automatically build the rest from that information. Hence, the constructor for our new `GameObject` class looks as follows:

```
GameObject(btCollisionShape* pShape, float mass, const btVector3
    &color, const btVector3 &initialPosition = btVector3(0,0,0),
    const btQuaternion &initialRotation = btQuaternion());
```

`GameObject` is a new class that stores important personal data, such as the Bullet object components, and its own color. It also gives us a few helper functions to access this data if we need (and we will). The majority of the work happens in the constructor, requiring us to specify the object's mass, color, shape, and initial transform (in the form of a vector for position and a quaternion for rotation).

Most of the code should be straightforward, with the exception of local inertia. This value is normally referred to as the **moment of inertia** in most physics circles. It essentially boils down to the object's resistance to change in angular velocity around each axis of rotation. The classic example of this is a pole carried by a tight rope walker. Because the pole is very long, it resists rotation allowing them to use it to maintain balance.

We have a special case built in to this function. If we define the mass to be zero, we also set the local inertia to (0,0,0). This will prevent the object from rotating as a result of collisions. In addition, Bullet uses a mass of zero to imply that you really want it to have an infinite mass, and hence don't want the object to move as result of forces like gravity. This is useful for environmental objects that don't move, such as a ground planes walls, and so on.

The **center of mass (COM)** of an object is an important property in Newtonian physics and it's just as important in physics simulations. Bullet will assume that the rigid body's COM is equal to its world position, unless told otherwise. Shifting the COM to some other location can be achieved through the usage of compound shapes, which will be explored more in *Chapter 7, Collision Shapes*.

Rendering our objects

We also need a more universal system to render our objects: one that chooses a different rendering function based on the type of object being rendered. The source code for this chapter now features a new DrawShape() function, which accepts a btCollisionShape pointer of any derived type, determines which type of shape it is using some of Bullet's internal enumerators, and then renders the appropriate shape.

> Since DrawBox() only covers boxes for now, we will be returning to this function later to expand on the additional shapes we introduce.

This change requires us to move the coloring and positioning of our objects (the glColor3f(), glPushMatrix(), and glPopMatrix() calls) out of DrawBox() and into DrawShape(), to spare us from duplicating the same instructions each time we render.

When a box is detected, through the BOX_SHAPE_PROXYTYPE enumerator, it gets the appropriate size for the box, by typecasting to btBoxShape and calling getHalfExtentsWithMargin(). This function returns the box's half size, or half the size in each direction. This value is convenient for collision-response mathematics, and since boxes are symmetrical shapes, physics engines typically define boxes this way.

Storing our objects

Picking the correct data structure for our needs is a matter of determining our requirements and matching them to the properties of the various kinds of data structures available. Tasks such as updating/rendering require quick iteration, since there could be a very long list of world objects we need to check through. Meanwhile, we're not particularly worried about tasks such as random access, or insertion and deletion since these will be fairly rare tasks to perform.

For quick iteration, you can't do much better than one of the array based data structures (of which there are many). A dynamic array or vector (not to be confused with the 3D math variety of vector) should suit us well for our game objects. Although, keep in mind that dynamic arrays are not the most efficient at random access, insertion, or deletion.

There's a common saying in software engineering that *preoptimization is the root of all evil*. Don't spend too much time thinking about the perfect data structure to use (or heaven forbid, building it all from scratch). It's wise to just get your application working first, then go back and optimize if and only if you find out that they turn out to be a significant bottleneck once you begin profiling. You may find that your choice of data structure doesn't matter at all, because there could be bigger optimization problems popping up in areas you never even considered.

The **Standard Template Library** (**STL**) is a library that comes standard with most C++ compilers, particularly Visual Studio. This library is enormous and contains classes and tools to handle many different, common problems that C++ programmers come across. It also contains a collection of useful data structures that we can use to store the objects such as our GameObject. A simple STL vector should be sufficient for this task:

```
typedef std::vector<GameObject*> GameObjects;
GameObjects m_objects;
```

This allows us to refer to our vector using a custom GameObjects type, instead of using the ugly namespace/template combination each time.

Consequently this allows us to replace our main rendering code with the following:

```
void BulletOpenGLApplication::RenderScene() {
  // create an array of 16 floats (representing a 4x4 matrix)
  btScalar transform[16];
```

```
    // iterate through all of the objects in our world
    for(GameObjects::iterator i = m_objects.begin(); i !=
      m_objects.end(); ++i) {
      // get the object from the iterator
      GameObject* pObj = *i;
      // read the transform
      pObj->GetTransform(transform);
      // get data from the object and draw it
      DrawShape(transform, pObj->GetShape(), pObj->GetColor());
    }
  }
```

Having our objects stored in a data structure like this provides a lot more flexibility to add new objects to our scene without undue effort.

As an interesting side note, Bullet uses a concept called **Single Instruction, Multiple Data (SIMD)** on some platforms, which makes the ability to run the same instruction on multiple pieces of data very rapid. In order to use this, the objects must be aligned in memory in steps of 16 bytes, and an STL vector does not naturally do this.

However, there is a built-in object type in Bullet called btAlignedObjectArray, which functions similarly to an STL vector and is worth exploring if you wish to make use of performance enhancements like SIMD in the future. Iterating through a large list of game objects and performing updates on them is a perfect situation to apply this technique.

Creating our objects

With our new system in place, we can introduce a new function to handle the creation of a GameObject for us. This function can be examined in the chapter's source code, but to summarize, it gathers the shape, mass, color, position, and rotation of the object we want to create, generates a new GameObject for it, and adds it to our dynamic array. As long as GameObject remains in the array, it will be automatically rendered in each step, greatly simplifying the act of adding new objects.

With this new function, we easily create our original box with the following call:

```
CreateGameObject(new btBoxShape(btVector3(1,1,1)), 1.0,
  btVector3(1.0f, 0.2f, 0.2f), btVector3(0.0f, 10.0f, 0.0f));
```

But, we can create two new objects with two more calls, and the majority of the work is taken care of by GameObject, RenderScene(), and DrawShape().

```
// create a ground plane
CreateGameObject (new btBoxShape(btVector3(1,50,50)), 0,
  btVector3(0.2f, 0.6f, 0.6f), btVector3(0.0f, 0.0f, 0.0f));
// create a second box
CreateGameObject (new btBoxShape(btVector3(1,1,1)), 1.0,
  btVector3(0.0f, 0.2f, 0.8f), btVector3(1.25f, 20.0f, 0.0f));
```

 Note that the increasing values of x in the initial position means the object starts further left. This is because of the position of our camera relative to the objects.

Now if we run our application, we should see a blue box falling down, hitting the red box, tilting, and falling over. It took us only two extra lines of code to create two new objects; that's a pretty good effort-to-reward ratio! The following screenshot shows our application with our new ground plane, and a new box colliding with our original box:

Debug rendering

Observing a problem visually is usually the easiest first step in diagnosing it. So it is helpful for a physics engine to provide a means to draw debug information onto the screen whether it's the edges of objects, the points of collision, the depth of penetration, or more. Bullet provides a very simple interface for us to render this kind of debugging data onto our scene, which we will implement in this section.

 Continue from here using the `Chapter4.2_DebugDrawer` project files.

Building the debug drawer

To create our own debug drawer, we will inherit from `btIDebugDraw`, an interface class for debug rendering. This object must override essential functions such as `drawLine()` or `drawContactPoint()`. There are a few functions such as `reportErrorWarning()` and `draw3dText()` that we're not interested in, but are pure virtual, and requires us to at least define them. Since we won't need them, we will leave them empty.

Here is a snippet of one of the functions defined in `DebugDrawer`, which draws a colored line between the two given points:

```
void DebugDrawer::drawLine(const btVector3 &from,const btVector3
   &to, const btVector3 &color)
{
  // draws a simple line of pixels between points.
  // use the GL_LINES primitive to draw lines
  glBegin(GL_LINES);
  glColor3f(color.getX(), color.getY(), color.getZ());
  glVertex3f(from.getX(), from.getY(), from.getZ());
  glVertex3f(to.getX(), to.getY(), to.getZ());
  glEnd();
}
```

The `DebugDrawer` class must be handed over to the world object through a call to `setDebugDrawer()`. In each render call, we will ask the world object to render the debug information through a call to `debugDrawWorld()`. This will cause the world to determine what needs to be rendered, based on which debug flags are set in `m_debugFlags`, and leave the actual rendering to our `DebugDrawer` class. Note that the only reason it can accept and use it is because it was derived from the `btIDebugDraw` interface class. If this seems confusing, it's worth brushing up on the concepts of **Polymorphism**.

The following is a snippet from the `Keyboard()` function, which allows us to change a single debug flag. These flags must come from Bullet's own internal enumerator of values, since it uses this to decide what to render for us.

```
case 'w':
  // toggle wireframe debug drawing
  m_pDebugDrawer->ToggleDebugFlag(btIDebugDraw::DBG_DrawWireframe);
  break;
```

Now our application can render debug lines and AABB volumes through a press of *W* or *B*, respectively. The following screenshot shows the application with debug rendering enabled:

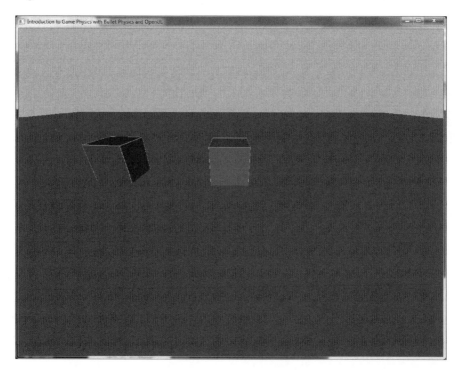

Introducing activation states

It may be apparent that the wireframe color of our boxes changes from white to green a few moments after an object comes to rest. This is yet another optimization that Bullet handles internally, which is only visualized through the debug mode, but has a profound effect on CPU usage. Objects whose velocity is below a given threshold for a given amount of time have their activation state set to deactivated. Meanwhile, there are actually two dynamic bounding volume trees created when you use a `btDbvtBroadphase` object (as we did). One stores the active objects (the active tree), and the other stores any static or deactivated objects (the deactive tree). So, when an object is deactivated, it pushes them into the other tree.

This causes Bullet to skip over them when its time for the world to move objects around, and since the broad phase object only compares the active tree against itself, and the active tree against the deactive tree (more importantly, it doesn't compare the deactive tree against the deactive tree) its impact on processing time is reduced even further. Later, when an active object collides with the deactivated one, it is activated once more, pushed back into the active tree, and Bullet performs the necessary calculations until it decides to deactivate it once more. These activation/deactivation states are typically referred to as putting the object to sleep, or waking it up.

 Note that the ground plane is always drawn with a green wireframe (asleep) because Bullet knows that this object has an infinite mass, is static, is never a part of the active tree, and thus will never need to be moved.

This optimization has its drawbacks; sometimes an object may be moving slow intentionally, but if it is moving too slowly, Bullet deactivates it. For example, we might have an object that is very slowly teetering on an edge, which means it has a very low angular velocity for a long time, at which point Bullet may assume that it needs to put the object to sleep. This can cause some bizarre situations, where an object looks like it should be falling over, but is in fact it is frozen in place at an angle that would not be possible in the real world.

The typical workaround is to tweak the sleep threshold of the object, the minimum values of linear and angular velocity, which Bullet considers too low. This can be achieved by calling `setSleepingThresholds()` on any rigid body. As a last resort, we can force all the objects to remain activated, by calling the `setActivationState(DISABLE_DEACTIVATION)` function on every new object, but this will cost us some performance, since every object will now be a part of the active tree, and hence will be checked every iteration.

The domino effect

While on the subject of activation states, it is worth mentioning the **domino effect**. It is possible for entire groups of touching objects (often called **islands**) to be put to sleep in the same fashion, greatly reducing their impact on the CPU. Once Bullet detects that none of the objects has moved in a while, they will all be put to sleep eventually.

This might seem convenient and allow us to throw more objects into the simulation, but be warned. When these islands get too large, consisting of too many objects, all it takes is for one of them to be nudged and the entire stack could become active simultaneously as they collide with one another, wake one another up, and the entire simulation slows to a crawl until Bullet puts some or all of them back to sleep again.

Too much activity such as this occurring in too short span of time can lead to adverse physics simulation behavior sometimes known as the **Spiral of Death**. This occurs when the simulation takes more time processing the current step, than the step simulates; for example, if we take 20 ms to simulate a 16 ms timestep we're behind by 4 ms, so the simulation needs to compensate in the next step, requiring even more time to process.

This can create a situation of progressively lower and lower frame rates until the simulation finds enough breathing room (simulation steps where very little is going on, such as when the awoken island has finally been dealt with) to catch up to the current moment in time. This would obviously create a very jarring and disappointing gameplay experience.

However, as mentioned towards the end of *Chapter 3, Physics Initialization*, Bullet lets you deal with this situation by tweaking the second and third parameters of `stepSimulation()`. But, this information is worth keeping in mind if you use an alternative physics engine, or find yourself building a custom solution in the future.

An old, but still relevant, blog post covers this concept in more detail and suggests good methods to avoid it:

`http://gafferongames.com/game-physics/fix-your-timestep/`

Summary

We have introduced some generic object management code to better facilitate future projects and expansion. Our GameObject class contains the object data, while BulletOpenGLApplication ensures our objects are stored, and rendered regardless of how many we create and what their private properties might be.

We have also added debug rendering to our scene, so that we can visualize some of the information coming from our physics objects. This is a useful tool to keep in one's tool chest when working with a physics engine such as Bullet, since attempting to debug complex mathematics at a low level can be mind-bendingly difficult.

In the next chapter, we will implement some advanced mouse control through the power of raycasting and constraints.

Raycasting and Constraints

5

Many games use a mouse or touch screen as the primary means of controlling objects; whether it's by selecting, moving, creating, or destroying them.

If we want to implement such a system into our application, then we must find a way to translate a mouse click (x-y coordinates on the screen) into a method of detecting the first object underneath the pointer. The answer to this conundrum is **raycasting**, which we will be exploring in this chapter.

Then, once we have a raycasting system in place, we will explore how we can use it in combination with Bullet's constraint system to move objects with the mouse cursor.

The power of raycasting

Raycasting is a technique that can be used for a variety of different tasks. A common use is to find objects underneath the cursor from the camera's perspective. This is typically referred to as **picking**. However, rays are also used in other tasks, such as in shooter games to cast a line from the barrel of a weapon to where a bullet might strike, which could be a wall or another player.

Another common usage of rays is to surround a player character with many rays that point outwards from the object, that are used as feelers to detect if the player is near other objects. For example, there could be a ray that points downwards from the player's feet a short distance. If the ray collides with a physical object, then we know that the player is touching the ground and telling us to play the appropriate animation, or reset a flag that allows them to jump.

Regardless, all of these concepts are built from the same basic idea; choose a starting point, pick a direction to travel in (a ray), and move along that direction (cast) until it collides with something. Let's create a basic picking ray function which exactly does that.

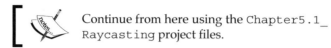

Continue from here using the `Chapter5.1_Raycasting` project files.

Picking rays

The `GetPickingRay()` function in the book's source code involves a large smattering of 3D mathematics that are beyond the scope of this book. It should be enough to know that it takes the x-y coordinates of a mouse click, and uses the camera's data (its position, near plane, far plane, field of view, and aspect ratio) to calculate and return a `btVector3` in world coordinates that points forward from the camera in the corresponding direction. If the camera moves, or we click somewhere else on the screen, then we get a new `btVector3` pointing forward from that position instead. Armed with this function, we can add some simple code to create a new object whenever we click on the right mouse button. This code can be found in the chapter's source code, in the `ShootBox()` function. This function is called by the `Mouse()` function anytime when the application detects that the right mouse button was clicked.

Recall that the `Mouse()` function was called by FreeGLUT anytime a mouse button is clicked. It gives us the button, the state (pressed or released), and the x-y coordinates of the click.

Launch our application and try right-clicking on the mouse. It should create a purple box and launch it towards the mouse cursor. The following screenshot shows this in action:

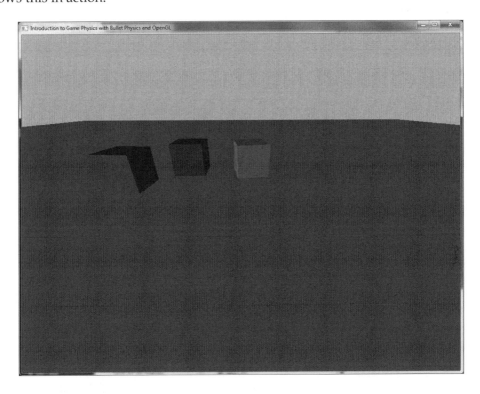

We've jumped ahead a little with the `setLinearVelocity()` function. This instruction is used to set the collision object's linear velocity. We'll learn more about manipulating the rigid bodies through functions such as this in *Chapter 6, Events, Triggers, and Explosions*.

Destroying objects

So far, we've essentially created a starting point for a picking ray. It is not a true raycast or picking ray until the ray travels forward in space and performs some type of collision detection. To destroy an object in our scene, we'll need to use our picking ray to perform a raycast and tell us the first rigid body with which it collides.

Raycasting in Bullet is handled through the btDynamicsWorld object's rayTest() function. We provide the starting point (as a btVector3), the direction (btVector3), and an object to store the raycast data inside, which should be one of two different classes that inherit from RayResultCallback. The object could either be:

- ClosestRayResultCallback, which gives the closest collision that the ray detected from the start location

- AllHitsRayResultCallback, which gives an array filled with all of the collisions the ray detected

Which object we want to use will depend on whether we want only the closest hit, or all of them. We will be using ClosestRayResultCallback, which contains useful data and member functions for the collision point, such as:

- hasHit(), which returns a boolean value and tells us if there was a collision between the ray and any physics object

- m_collisionObject, which is the btCollisionObject our ray hit

- m_hitPointWorld, which is the coordinate in world space where the ray detected a collision

The Raycast() function in the book's source code takes a picking ray and an empty output RayResult structure, uses it to create a ClosestRayResultCallback, and then performs a raycast test. If the raycast was successful, the function fills out the structure and returns true, allowing us to check the success or failure of the raycast outside of this function.

 Notice the special case to avoid picking static objects, such as our ground plane. When we gave our ground plane a mass of zero, Bullet automatically set the static flag for us, allowing us to check for it at a later date.

Before we can destroy the picked rigid body we need to know what GameObject that corresponds to. We will have to search through our list of game objects, comparing their rigid bodies with the picked one, until we find it. Then, and only then, is it safe to destroy it.

Check the `DestroyGameObject()` function in the chapter's source code for details of this process. This function searches through our list of objects hunting down `GameObject` that corresponds to the given `btRigidBody`. It is then called during the `Keyboard()` function, whenever we detect that the user pressed the *D* key.

> Note that the mouse coordinates, x and y, are also passed into functions such as `Keyboard()`. This greatly simplifies our input handling, preventing us from having to store the current mouse data locally.

Launch the application, hover the mouse cursor over an object, and press *D* on the keyboard. Any objects beneath the cursor should now be instantly destroyed (with the exception of the ground plane). The following are the screenshots before and after destruction of the box on the left:

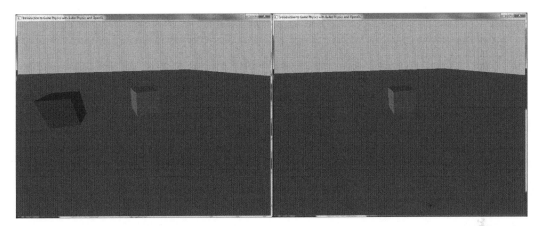

Constraints

We'll now explore Bullet's constraint feature. These objects limit the range of motion of one object relative to another, giving us the power to create some very interesting and unique gameplay situations.

> Continue from here using the `Chapter5.2_ Constraints` project files.

Understanding constraints

Constraints, in their most basic form, are the rules which limit the range of motion of an object relative to some specific object or point in space. For example, think of a desk chair. It is made up of multiple parts, but if we push the base of the chair, the rest must move with it. The same happens if we push the top section; so even though the chair is made of multiple pieces, they are constrained to one another by a handful of rules.

Constraints can be used to also simulate the independent rotation of the desk chair's top section relative to the base. The top section is able to rotate around an axis without any dependence on what the bottom section is doing. This constraint is simulated by hooking the top section to an invisible point, and only allowing rotation around a single axis about that point.

Constraints can vary in how strongly they influence their target objects. A strong constraint enforces its limitation on movement at all times as strongly as it can. So, if two objects are connected by a very strong, rigid constraint, it is the equivalent of being attached together by invisible and unbreakable glue. In other words, if one object is moved one unit in space, then the other must move one unit in space to follow it.

Weaker constraints are more like springs. Under the same scenario, the first object might move one unit in space, but the second moves somewhat less, causing the two objects to come closer together, or pushed further apart. In addition, the more they are pushed away from their resting position, the harder the constraint pulls them back; if we recall our Newtonian physics, this is much like how a simple spring functions.

Picking up objects

A feature of most games is to allow the player to pick up and move the objects around with the mouse cursor or touch screen (also useful for debugging and testing!). There are several ways to achieve this, such as with forces, or updating the rigid body's transform each iteration, but we would like to use a constraint to achieve this effect.

The idea is to use our existing raycasting functionality to detect which object was selected and the exact point of a mouse click. We then create a new constraint at that point and attach it to the selected object. Then, every time we move the mouse (while the mouse button is still held down), we update the position of the constraint. The expectation being that our selected object would move with the constraint, and keep the same relative position until it is freed from its influence.

There are a handful of different objects which Bullet provides in order to implement the constraint system. We'll cover the `btGenericDof6Constraint` object, the most generic of the available options (hence the name). Its purpose is to give us an interface to limit the six degrees of freedom (*Dof6* for short) of an object; these refer to the three axes of both linear and angular motion. This constraint can either be used to hook two rigid bodies together, or hook a single object to a single point in space.

Building a constraint

We've seen raycasting in action earlier in this chapter, so all we need to cover is the creation, update, and destruction of the constraint itself. `CreatePickingConstraint()` is a very large function, so we'll explore some code snippets one step at a time:

```
if (!Raycast(m_cameraPosition, GetPickingRay(x, y), output))
    return;
```

This instruction should look familiar, since we used it earlier in this chapter. It performs a raycast and returns true if it finds anything, pushing the relevant data into the output variable.

```
m_pPickedBody->setActivationState(DISABLE_DEACTIVATION);
```

Here we're ensuring the picked object doesn't fall asleep while attached to our constraint. We covered activation states back in *Chapter 4*, *Object Management and Debug Rendering* and the last thing we want is our picked object to freeze in place while we still have it selected!

```
// get the hit position relative to the body we hit
btVector3 localPivot = m_pPickedBody-
    >getCenterOfMassTransform().inverse() * output.hitPoint;
```

We mentioned earlier how we would create the constraint at the exact point of the click, which is exactly what the previous calls do, except it does so in a rather convoluted way.

Constraints must be defined in local space coordinates, for example, let's say we have two objects positioned at (0,3,0) and (0,10,0) in world space coordinates. But, from the first object's perspective, it is always positioned at (0,0,0) in its own local space, regardless of where it is in world space. Also, as far as the first box is concerned, the other box is positioned at (0,7,0) in its local space. Meanwhile, from the second object's perspective, it is also positioned at (0,0,0) in its local space, and the other box is located at (0,-7,0) in its local space.

It's possible to obtain these values mathematically by multiplying the vector representing a point in world space by the inverse of an object's transformation matrix. Therefore in the preceding code, we multiply the hit point by the inverse transform of the box's center of mass, giving us the hit point coordinates from the box's local space perspective.

 The previous mathematical calculation is a very important and useful feature of matrices that is worth remembering for the future.

Next we create our constraint object:

```
btGeneric6DofConstraint* dof6 = new
    btGeneric6DofConstraint(*m_pPickedBody, pivot, true);
```

The constraint requires us to provide the body in question, the pivot point (again, in local space coordinates), and a `bool` value. This boolean tells the constraint whether to store various pieces of data relative to object A (the rigid body) or object B (the constraint's pivot point in this case, but could also be a second rigid body). This becomes important when using the constraint later.

```
dof6->setAngularLowerLimit(btVector3(0,0,0));
dof6->setAngularUpperLimit(btVector3(0,0,0));
```

Also, calling the `setAngularUpperLimit()` and `setAngularLowerLimit()` functions with zero's `btVector3`s add a rotational limitation to the box while it is attached to this constraint, preventing it from rotating.

```
m_pWorld->addConstraint(dof6,true);
```

Much like rigid bodies, it's not enough to create the object; we must also inform the world of its existence, hence we call the `addConstraint()` function. The second parameter disables the collisions between the two linked bodies. Since we don't have two bodies in this constraint (we have a body and a pivot point), it would be wise to tell Bullet to save itself some effort by setting the value to `true`. If we had two rigid bodies connected via a weak constraint and were interested in having them collide, we would want to set this value to `false`.

```
// define the 'strength' of our constraint (each axis)
float cfm = 0.5f;
dof6->setParam(BT_CONSTRAINT_STOP_CFM,cfm,0);
dof6->setParam(BT_CONSTRAINT_STOP_CFM,cfm,1);
dof6->setParam(BT_CONSTRAINT_STOP_CFM,cfm,2);
dof6->setParam(BT_CONSTRAINT_STOP_CFM,cfm,3);
dof6->setParam(BT_CONSTRAINT_STOP_CFM,cfm,4);
```

```
dof6->setParam(BT_CONSTRAINT_STOP_CFM,cfm,5);
// define the 'error reduction' of our constraint (each axis)
float erp = 0.5f;
dof6->setParam(BT_CONSTRAINT_STOP_ERP,erp,0);
dof6->setParam(BT_CONSTRAINT_STOP_ERP,erp,1);
dof6->setParam(BT_CONSTRAINT_STOP_ERP,erp,2);
dof6->setParam(BT_CONSTRAINT_STOP_ERP,erp,3);
dof6->setParam(BT_CONSTRAINT_STOP_ERP,erp,4);
dof6->setParam(BT_CONSTRAINT_STOP_ERP,erp,5);
```

This is where things get a little weird. The `setParam()` function sets the value of a number of different constraint variables, two of which are used in the preceding code. It is called a total of twelve times, since there are three axes, two directions for each axis (positive and negative), and two different types of variable to edit (3x2x2 = 12). The two aforementioned variables are **CFM (Constraint Force Mixing)** and **ERP (Error Reduction Parameter)**.

CFM is essentially a measure of the strength of the constraint. A value of 0 means a perfectly rigid constraint, while increasing values make the constraint more spring like, up to a value of 1 where it has no effect at all.

ERP represents the fraction of how much joint error will be used in the next simulation step. Many constraints could be working in unison to create a complex interaction (imagine a rope bridge, which can be simulated by a attaching a bunch of springs connected together) and ERP is used to determine how much of the previous data will affect the calculation of future data. This is a difficult concept to explain in such a short space, but imagine that we have multiple constraints acting on the same object, each forcing the others into breaking their own rules. ERP is then the priority of this constraint relative to the others, and helps determine who has higher importance during these types of complex constraint scenarios.

And there we have it. We detected the collision point, and then built our constraint. That wasn't so bad, was it? The last snippet of code to look at is in the `Motion()` function, the code which updates the position of the constraint while we're still holding down the left mouse button.

```
// use another picking ray to get the target direction
btVector3 dir = GetPickingRay(x,y) - m_cameraPosition;
dir.normalize();
// use the same distance as when we originally picked the object
dir *= m_oldPickingDist;
btVector3 newPivot = m_cameraPosition + dir;
// set the position of the constraint
pickCon->getFrameOffsetA().setOrigin(newPivot);
```

It was mentioned earlier that it was possible to get data from the constraint in a form which is relative to one of the two objects involved in the constraint (called A and B). We use the `getFrameOffsetA()` function to get the transform position of the constraint relative to the first object, and then update it with the new value. This is the equivalent to updating the position of the constraint's pivot point. Thus in the next simulation step, the constraint will attempt to move the box to the new position of the mouse, keeping the same distance from the camera as when it was first picked.

The last thing to mention is the `RemovePickingConstraint()` function, which makes sure that we have an existing constraint before attempting to destroy it. If so, we must remove it from the world, destroy the object in memory, nullify the pointers. The re-enable the ability of the picked up object to go back to sleep.

In this section's application we can pick up one of our objects with the left mouse button and move it around. The following screenshot shows that the first box has been moved on top of the second box of to our mouse clicking constraint:

Try tweaking the `bLimitAngularMotion`, `cfm`, and `erp` variables in `CreatePickingConstraint()` and observe the effects they have on the picked object.

Summary

We've witnessed the power of picking, raycasting, and constraints by adding some mouse control to our application. This flexible system is used to create, move, and destroy objects in the scene. This allows for some very creative gameplay mechanics, animations, and effects, since many games rely on these mechanisms as an essential component of gameplay, so these are all lessons to take forward when implementing similar systems in your own projects.

In the next chapter, we'll add more game logic control to our application by adding a collision event system, complete with volumes of space which act as triggers, and manipulating our objects through various types of force.

6
Events, Triggers, and Explosions

Almost every game needs some form of event system that informs the game logic about collisions that have occurred between objects, and many of these events are triggered by invisible volumes of space that react when certain game objects enter them. In this chapter, we'll learn how to build these features and then apply them by simulating an explosion!

Building a collision event system

In a game such as Angry Birds, we would want to know when a breakable object such as a pig or piece of wood has collided with something, so that we can determine the amount of damage that was dealt, and whether or not the object should be destroyed, which in turn spawns some particle effects and increments the player's score.

It's the game logic's job to distinguish between the objects, but it's the physics engine's responsibility to send these events in the first place and then we can extract this information from Bullet through its **persistent manifolds**.

Continue from here using the `Chapter6.1_CollisionEvents` project files.

Explaining the persistent manifolds

Persistent manifolds are the objects that store information between pairs of objects that pass the broad phase. If we remember our physics engine theory from *Chapter 3, Physics Initialization*, the broad phase returns a shortlist of the object pairs that might be touching, but are not necessarily touching. They could still be a short distance apart from one another, so the existence of a manifold does not imply a collision. Once you have the manifolds, there's still a little more work to do to verify if there is a collision between the object pair.

One of the most common mistakes made with the Bullet physics engine is to assume that the existence of a manifold is enough to signal a collision. This results in detecting collision events a couple of frames too early (while the objects are still approaching one another) and detecting separation events too late (once they've separated far enough away that they no longer pass the broad phase). This often results in a desire to blame Bullet for being sluggish, when the fault lies with the user's original assumptions. Be warned!

Manifolds reside within the collision dispatcher (a core Bullet object we created back in *Chapter 3, Physics Initialization*), and Bullet keeps the same manifolds in memory for as long as the same object pairs keep passing the broad phase. This is useful if you want to keep querying the same contact information between pairs of objects over time. This is where the persistent part comes in, which serves to optimize the memory allocation process by minimizing how often the manifolds are created and destroyed.

Bullet is absolutely riddled with subtle optimizations and this is just one of them. This is all the more reason to use a known good physics solution like Bullet, instead of trying to take on the world and building your own!

The manifold class in question is `btPersistentManifold` and we can gain access to the manifold list through the collision dispatcher's `getNumManifolds()` and `getManifoldByIndexInternal()` functions.

Each manifold contains a handful of different functions and member variables to make use of, but the ones we're most interested in for now are `getBody0()`, `getBody1()`, and `getNumContacts()`. These functions return the two bodies in the object pair that passed the broad phase, and the number of contacts detected between them. We will use these functions to verify if a collision has actually taken place, and send the involved objects through an event.

Managing the collision event

There are essentially two ways to handle collision events: either send an event every update while two objects are touching (and continuously while they're still touching), or send events both when the objects collide and when the objects separate.

In almost all cases it is wiser to pick the latter option, since it is simply an optimized version of the first. If we know when the objects start and stop touching, then we can assume that the objects are still touching between those two moments in time. So long as the system also informs us of peculiar cases in separation (such as if one object is destroyed, or teleports away while they're still touching), then we have everything we need for a collision event system.

Bullet strives to be feature-rich, but also flexible, allowing us to build custom solutions to problems such as this; so this feature is not built into Bullet by default. In other words, we will need to build this logic ourselves. Our goals are simple; determine if a pair of objects have either collided or separated during the step, and if so, broadcast the corresponding event. The basic process is as follows:

1. For each manifold, check if the two objects are touching (the number of contact points will be greater than zero).
2. If so, add the pair to a list of pairs that we found in this step.
3. If the same pair was not detected during the previous step, broadcast a collision event.
4. Once we've finished checking the manifolds, create another list of collision objects that contains only the missing collision pairs between the previous step and this step.
5. For each pair that is missing, broadcast a separation event.
6. Overwrite the list of collision pairs from the previous step, with the list we created for this step.

There are several **STL (Standard Template Library)** objects and functions we can use to make these steps easier. An `std::pair` can be used to store the objects in pairs, and can be stored within an `std::set`. These sets let us perform rapid comparisons between two sets using a helpful function, `std::set_difference()`. This function tells us the elements that are present in the first set, but not in the second.

The following diagram shows how `std::set_difference` returns only objects pairs that are present in the first set, but missing from the second set. Note that it does not return new object pairs from the second set.

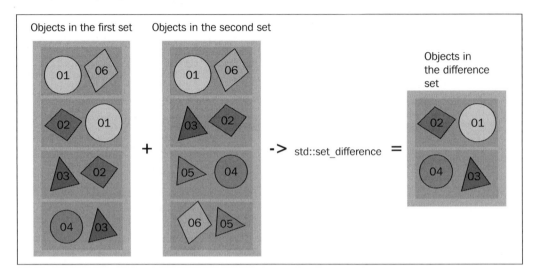

The most important function introduced in this chapter's source code is `CheckForCollisionEvents()`. The code may look a little intimidating at first, but it simply implements the steps listed previously. The comments should help us to identify each step.

When we detect a collision or separation, we will want some way to inform the game logic of it. These two functions will do the job nicely:

```
virtual void CollisionEvent(btRigidBody* pBody0, btRigidBody *
    pBody1);
virtual void SeparationEvent(btRigidBody * pBody0, btRigidBody *
    pBody1);
```

In order to test this feature, we introduce the following code to turn colliding objects white (and similar code to turn separating objects black):

```
void BulletOpenGLApplication::CollisionEvent(const
    btCollisionObject * pBody0, const btCollisionObject * pBody1) {
    GameObject* pObj0 = FindGameObject((btRigidBody*)pBody0);
    pObj0->SetColor(btVector3(1.0,1.0,1.0));
    GameObject* pObj1 = FindGameObject((btRigidBody*)pBody1);
    pObj1->SetColor(btVector3(1.0,1.0,1.0));
}
```

Note that these color changing commands are commented out in future project code.

When we launch the application, we should expect colliding and separating objects to change to the colors give in `CollisionEvent()`. Colliding objects should turn white, and separated objects should turn black. But, when objects have finished moving, we observe something that might seem a little counterintuitive. The following screenshot shows the two objects colored differently once they come to rest:

But, if we think about the order of events for a moment, it begins to make sense:

- When the first box collides with the ground plane, this turns both objects (the box and the ground plane) white.

- The second box then collides with the first turning the second box white, while the first box stays white.

- Next, the second box separates from the first box, meaning both objects turn black.

- Finally, the second box collides with the ground plane, turning the box white once again.

What was the last color that the first box turned to? The answer is black, because the last event it was involved in was a separation with the second box. But, how can the box be black if it's touching something? This is an intentional design consequence of this particular style of collision event management; one where we only recognize the collision and separation events.

If we wanted objects to remember that they're still touching something, we would have to introduce some internal method of counting how many objects they're still in contact with, and incrementing/decrementing the count each time a collision or separation event comes along. This naturally consumes a little memory and processing time, but it's certainly far more optimized than the alternative of spamming a new collision event every step while two objects are still touching. We want to avoid wasting CPU cycles telling ourselves information that we already know.

The `CollisionEvent()` and `SeparationEvent()` functions can be used by a game logic to determine if, when, and how two objects have collided. Since they hand over the rigid bodies involved in the collision, we can determine all kinds of important physics information, such as the points of contact (where they hit), and the difference in velocity/impulse force of the two bodies (how hard they hit). From there we can construct pretty much whatever physics collision-related game logic we desire.

 Try picking up, or introducing more objects with the left/right mouse buttons, causing further separations and collisions until you get a feel for how this system works.

Building trigger volumes

Imagine we want an invisible volume of space, and when the player stumbles into it, it triggers a trap or a cutscene. This concept is used countlessly throughout modern games (in fact, it's difficult to think of one in the last decade that doesn't use them somewhere).

This effect is achieved in Bullet by simply disabling the contact responses for any given rigid body.

 Continue from here using the `Chapter6.2_TriggerVolumes` project files.

Disabling contact response

There is no specific class required to build a trigger volume, but there is an essential flag which we can apply to any object: CF_NO_CONTACT_RESPONSE. This flag disables all contact response, informing Bullet that it should not calculate any physical response when other objects collide with the flagged object. This does not prevent it from performing broad and narrow phase collision detection and informing us when an overlap occurs, hence our CollisionEvent() and CollisionSeparation() functions will still be called even for objects flagged in this way. The only difference is that other objects will pass through it unhindered.

Here's a snippet of code from BasicDemo::CreateObjects():

```
// create a trigger volume
m_pTrigger = new btCollisionObject();
// create a box for the trigger's shape
m_pTrigger->setCollisionShape(new btBoxShape(btVector3(1,0.25,1)));
// set the trigger's position
btTransform triggerTrans;
triggerTrans.setIdentity();
triggerTrans.setOrigin(btVector3(0,1.5,0));
m_pTrigger->setWorldTransform(triggerTrans);
// flag the trigger to ignore contact responses
m_pTrigger->setCollisionFlags(btCollisionObject::CF_NO_CONTACT_
RESPONSE);
// add the trigger to our world
m_pWorld->addCollisionObject(m_pTrigger);
```

The previous code creates a trigger volume hovering just above the ground plane. We don't want these trigger volumes to be rendered during runtime since these kinds of triggers usually remain invisible to the player. So we avoided using our CreateGameObject() function (which would have added it to the list of objects and automatically render it), and instead we built it manually.

However, even though it is invisible to the player, we can still observe it through the debug renderer. If we enable wireframe mode (the *W* key), Bullet will draw the shape for us so that we can visualize the trigger volume in the space.

Meanwhile, BasicDemo includes an override for CollisionEvent() which checks if the two objects involved are the box and the trigger, and if so, it spawns a large box besides it. Note that we don't necessarily know if pBody0 or pBody1 represents either object, so we need to check both pointers:

```
void BasicDemo::CollisionEvent(btRigidBody* pBody0, btRigidBody*
pBody1) {
```

```
    // did the box collide with the trigger?
    if (pBody0 == m_pBox->GetRigidBody() && pBody1 == m_pTrigger ||
      pBody1 == m_pBox->GetRigidBody() && pBody0 == m_pTrigger) {
      // if yes, create a big green box nearby
        CreateGameObject(new btBoxShape(btVector3(2,2,2)), 2.0,
    btVector3(0.3, 0.7, 0.3), btVector3(5, 10, 0));
    }
}
```

Launch the application, and enable wireframe debugging (the *W* key). We should see a trigger volume (denoted by a white wireframe) just below the spawn point of the first box. Moments after, the box should collide with the trigger, causing `CollisionEvent()` to be called. Since the two objects involved are the trigger volume, and the first box, the `if` statement will become true, and a new game object will be created. The following screenshot shows a new object (the large box) being spawned after the first box collides with the trigger volume:

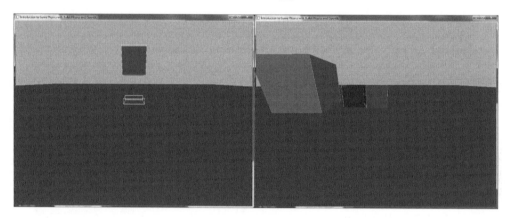

Force, torque, and impulse

Next, we will explore how to manipulate the motion of our collision objects through forces, torques, and impulses and also discuss the important differences between them.

[Continue from here using the `Chapter6.3_ForceTorqueAndImpulse` project files.]

Understanding the object motion

We have already observed one method of moving a rigid body with our `ShootBox()` command back in *Chapter 5, Raycasting and Constraints*, by calling the `setLinearVelocity()` function on the object's rigid body after creating it. This function sets the magnitude and direction of the object's linear motion. Meanwhile, another commonly used motion altering command is `setAngularVelocity()`, which is used to set the object's rotational velocity.

However, simple velocity altering commands like these do not add much life or believability to a scene, since we humans are also familiar with the concept of acceleration due to effects such as gravity, or the inertia we feel when we drive a car, ride a bike, or even walk. Acceleration can be applied in Bullet through the use of forces. There are different types of force, where each one has some important distinctions that must be understood before making use of them. We'll discuss the following commands that are accessible through any `btRigidBody`:

- `applyForce()`
- `applyTorque()`
- `applyImpulse()`
- `applyTorqueImpulse()`
- `applyCentralForce()`
- `applyCentralImpulse()`

All of the preceding functions require a `btVector3` object to define the direction and the strength of the effect. Just like the Newtonian definition, forces (such as gravity) continuously accelerate an object in a given direction, but do not affect their rotation. Meanwhile, torque is the rotational equivalent of a force, applying a rotational acceleration to an object causing it to rotate in place around its center of mass. Hence, `applyForce()` and `applyTorque()` provide the means for applying these effects, respectively.

Meanwhile, the difference between forces and impulses is that impulses are forces that are independent of time. For instance, if we applied a force to an object for a single step, the resultant acceleration on that object would depend on how much time had passed during that step. Thus, two computers running at slightly different time steps would see two completely different resultant velocities of the object after the same action. This would be very bad for a networked game, and equally bad for a single player game that suffered a sudden spike in activity that increased the step time temporarily.

However, applying an impulse for a single step would give us the exact same result on both computers because the resultant velocity is calculated without any dependence on time. Thus, if we want to apply an instantaneous force, it is better to use applyImpulse(). Whereas, if we want to move objects over several iterations, then it is better to use applyForce(). Similarly, applying a *Torque Impulse* is an identical concept, except it applies a rotational impulse. Hence, we would use applyTorqueImpulse() if we wanted an instantaneous rotational kick.

Finally, the difference between applyCentralForce() and applyForce() is simply that the former always applies the force to the center of mass of the object, while the latter requires us to provide a position relative to the center of mass (which could always default to the center of mass, anyway). Basically, the Central functions are there for convenience, while the rest are more flexible since in the real world if we pushed a box on its edge we would expect it to move linearly (force), but also rotate a little (torque) as it moved. The same distinction applies to applyCentralImpulse() and applyImpulse().

Knowing all of this, if we follow the pattern of function names we may notice that applyCentralTorque() is missing. This is because there's no such thing in the laws of physics. A torque must always be applied at an offset from the center of mass, since a central torque would simply be a linear force.

Applying forces

In the source code for this section, BasicDemo has been modified to grab the G key, and apply a force of 20 units in the y axis to the first box (the red one). This is strong enough to counteract the force of gravity (default of -10 in the y axis), and cause our object to accelerate upwards while the key is held down.

Check the Keyboard(), KeyboardUp(), and UpdateScene() functions of BasicDemo to see this process in action.

Note that each of the override functions used in this process begins by calling back to the base class implementation of the same function. This ensures that our base class code, which handles keyboard input and scene updating, is still called before we do anything unique in our derived class.

Launch our application and try pressing and holding the *G* key. Our first box should now begin to float. The following screenshot shows how our first box can be lifted up, land back in the trigger volume, and summon even more boxes:

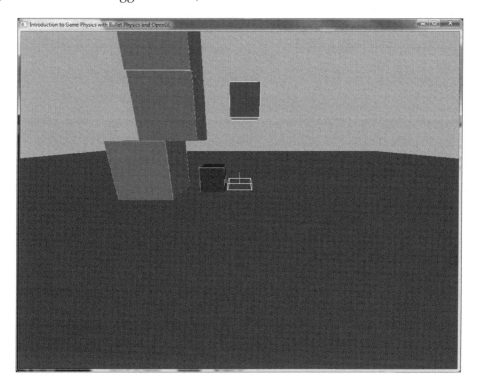

Also note that the lifted box may seem to rotate and veer off-course slightly even though we're always applying an upward force. Two effects contribute to this: the natural inaccuracy of floating point numbers and subtle differences in contact responses on each of the different vertices when the box hits the ground.

Applying impulses

Next, we'll work through an example of an impulse by creating a small explosive force at the location of the mouse cursor. In order to simulate an explosion, we will need to create a spherical trigger volume, instead of a box (since a box-shaped explosion would be really weird). When collisions are detected with this volume we can apply an impulse that points from the center of the explosion towards the target object(s), forcing the object away from its epicenter. However, we only want this object to linger for a single simulation step, so that we can tightly control the amount of acceleration applied to the target objects.

Since we want our explosion to be generated only temporarily when a key is pressed, this presents a problem when we interact with the Keyboard() command, since it is called once when a key is pressed, and continuously while the key is still held down. It's possible to tweak our input system to not repeat calls like this with a FreeGLUT function call (as mentioned previously in *Chapter 1, Building a Game Application*), but our camera moving code currently depends on the current style, so changing it now would cause a different set of problems.

So, what we can do is use a simple Boolean flag that tells us if we can create an explosion object. When we want to create an explosion, we will check if the flag is true. If so, we create the explosion and set the flag to false, and we will not set the flag back to true again until the key is released. This prevents subsequent calls to the Keyboard() function from creating another explosion trigger volume unless we detect a key up event.

This is a fairly straightforward process, and the source code for this chapter adds the relevant code to produce this effect with slight tweaks to the Keyboard(), KeyboardUp(), UpdateScene(), and CollisionEvent() functions of BasicDemo. The 3D math implemented in the code uses some simple vector arithmetic to obtain the final direction by converting the vector between them into a unit vector, and obtaining the final magnitude from the distance between the objects and some constant value (EXPLOSION_STRENGTH). With a direction and a magnitude, we can create our final impulse vector.

Launch the application, place the mouse cursor somewhere near the boxes, and press the *E* key. This will result in an invisible explosion that pushes all the nearby objects away through a simple impulse force. The following screenshot shows what happens when an explosion is generated between the boxes (epicenter and direction of travel added for artistic flair):

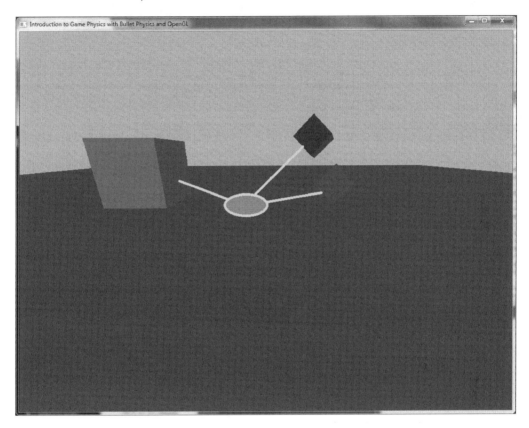

Note that to simulate the explosion a little more realistically, the strength of the explosion follows an inverse law, since we wouldn't expect an object further from the center to experience the same impulse as those that are near.

```
if (dist != 0.0) strength /= dist;
```

Also note that an additional parameter was added to the `Raycast()` function to allow us to decide whether we want it to return collisions with static objects or not (like the ground plane). These were ignored originally because we didn't want our `DestroyGameObject()` function to destroy the ground plane. But, now we need this special case in order to generate an explosion somewhere on the ground plane's edge; otherwise it would simply ignore them and we could only generate explosions on the edges of the boxes. It's set to `false` by default, to spare us from having to edit our existing calls to `Raycast()`.

```
bool Raycast(const btVector3 &startPosition, const btVector3
    &direction, RayResult &output, bool includeStatic = false);
```

Summary

Very little game logic can be built around a physics engine without a collision event system, so we made Bullet broadcast collision and separation events to our application so that it can be used by our game logic. This works by checking the list of manifolds, and creating logic that keeps track of important changes in these data structures.

Once we have these collision events, we need to do something with them, and we explored how to use a collision event between a box and an invisible trigger volume to instantiate a new object in our world, and how to capture these events within an instant of time when an explosion is generated.

In the next chapter, we will explore some of the more unusual types of collision shapes offered by Bullet.

7

Collision Shapes

So far we've only built box collision shapes, but Bullet offers much more variety than this. In this chapter, we'll explore some more built-in collision shapes to bring more variety into our scene. We will initially cover some more built-in shapes such as spheres and cylinders, and then explore how to build unique, customized shapes through convex hulls and compound shapes.

Spheres and cylinders

The btSphereShape and btCylinderShape are the two collision shapes that could not be more simple; they define a sphere and cylinder, respectively.

 Continue from here using the Chapter7.1_ SpheresAndCylinders project files.

We already know how to create btBoxShape, and building these new built-in shapes is not much different. Note that nothing about the way we handle rigid bodies or motion states changes when we start working with different collision shapes. This is one of the big advantages of the Bullet's modular object system. These new shapes can be instantiated in the creation of a new GameObject as follows:

```
CreateGameObject(new btSphereShape(1.0f), 1.0, btVector3(0.7f,
    0.7f, 0.0f), btVector3(-5.0, 10.0f, 0.0f));
CreateGameObject(new btCylinderShape(btVector3(1,1,1)), 1.0,
    btVector3(0.0f, 0.7f, 0.0f), btVector3(-2, 10.0f, 0.0f));
```

Simple, right? Unfortunately, we now face a more significant challenge: how to render these new objects? We could just render them like boxes, but this won't be ideal. We'll need to introduce some new drawing functions, akin to DrawBox(), which render objects of differing shapes and sizes. Thanks to the rigorous refactoring we performed on our rendering code back in *Chapter 4, Object Management and Debug Rendering*, we have made this whole process fairly trivial on ourselves.

DrawSphere() uses a new OpenGL primitive type, GL_QUAD_STRIP, to create strips of quads. A quad is made of four points, rather than three points for a triangle. A strip of quads is built two vertices at a time, since they are connected together in strips end-to-end. This is a much more efficient way of rendering many primitives in one step.

In order to generate a spherical object of a given radius with quads, we have to iterate laterally, find the angles of this segment, then iterate longitudinally, and draw them.

Meanwhile, to draw a cylinder we can make use of a new helper function in OpenGL to build the cylinder piece-by-piece using quadrics to build two disks via gluDisk(), and a cylindrical hull via gluCylinder(). These quadric functions are built into FreeGLUT, providing an interface with which we can build meshes using simple mathematical equations. There are various types of quadrics that are available in the FreeGLUT library, which you can find in the documentation and/or source code.

To save space we won't cover any code snippets here, since there are far too many bite-size simple commands being introduced. But, take the time to look at the new functions DrawSphere(), DrawCylinder(), and the changes to DrawShape().

Our application now renders a yellow sphere and green cylinder to accompany our two original boxes. Try shooting boxes at them and observe their motion. They behave exactly as we would expect a physics object of that shape to behave! The following screenshot shows our new cylindrical and spherical objects added to our scene:

Convex hulls

Next, we'll explore how Bullet lets us build custom collision shapes through the use of convex hulls.

 Continue from here using the `Chapter7.2_ConvexHulls` project files.

Much like our OpenGL code, we provide the vertex points from which to build the object and Bullet takes care of the hard work for us; in fact Bullet makes it even easier than that, because we don't need to define indices or provide them in a specific order of rotation. Bullet will always try to create the simplest convex shape it can from the given set of points (also known as a **point cloud** or **vertex cloud** in this context). It is important for the objects to be convex because it is orders of magnitude is easier to calculate collisions with convex shapes (those without any internal dips or caves in the shape) than with concave shapes (those with caves in its surface).

A convex hull is defined by the `btConvexHullShape` class. We must perform a little programming gymnastics to create our convex hull, by generating an array of five `btVector3`s, and passing the memory address of the first point's x coordinate into our convex hull. This may seem confusing at first, but it's straightforward once we appreciate the importance of contiguous memory.

A `btVector3` consists of four floats: x, y, z, and an unused buffer float. Why is there an unused variable in this object? Because CPUs are very efficient while working in powers of 2, and since a float is 4 bytes large, that makes an entire `btVector3` object 16 bytes large. Throwing in an unused float like this is a good way to force the compiled code to make these objects 16 bytes large. This is yet another one of those low-level optimizations to be found in Bullet. In addition, an array of `btVector3`s are contiguous in memory (by definition) such that they follow one another sequentially by address.

Point 1				Point 2				Point 3				Point 4				Point 5			
x	y	z	-	x	y	z	-	x	y	z	-	x	y	z	-	x	y	z	-
0	4	8	12	16	20	24	28	32	36	40	44	48	52	56	60	64	68	72	76

Five btVector3 objects contiguous in memory.

The `btConvexHullShape` constructor expects us to provide three things: the memory address of start of a list of vertex points, the number of vertices, and the stride, or how many bytes in memory it should jump to reach the next vertex.

Since the memory address must be provided in the form of `btScalar`, we will call `getX()` on the first point to get the memory address that we need. The number of vertices is required so that it knows when to stop counting (computers are stupid like that), and the stride is necessary to determine how to count. The default value for the stride is 16 bytes, which is (not by coincidence) the size of a `btVector3` object; so there's actually no need to provide this argument, but it is worth mentioning because this concept appears all the time when working with vertex and index buffers.

Hopefully things become clear once we explore the code for this procedure:

```
// create a vertex cloud defining a square-based pyramid
btVector3 points[5] = {btVector3(-0.5,1,1),
btVector3(-0.5,1,-1),
btVector3(-0.5,-1,1),
btVector3(-0.5,-1,-1),
btVector3(1,0,0)};
// create our convex hull
btConvexHullShape* pShape = new
  btConvexHullShape(&points[0].getX(),5);
// initialize the object as a polyhedron
pShape->initializePolyhedralFeatures();
// create the game object using our convex hull shape
CreateGameObject(pShape, 1.0, btVector3(1,1,1), btVector3(5, 15,
  0)));
```

There's one erroneous function call above, `initializePolyhedralFeatures()`. This function can be called on a convex hull shape to convert the data into a special format that gives us access to some convenient functions that we'll need to render the object later. It essentially builds the indices and vertices for us, so we don't have to.

Once again, we can throw this shape into our `GameObject` constructor and it is none the wiser. The only part of our code that cares is our rendering code. Once again we will skip providing the actual code here, but check out the new function `DrawConvexHull()` and changes to `DrawShape()` to observe the process of rendering these shapes. It is doing little more than grabbing the polyhedral vertex/index data and rendering the relevant triangles.

The following screenshot shows our application, which now includes a white pyramid shape falling from the sky along with our original shapes:

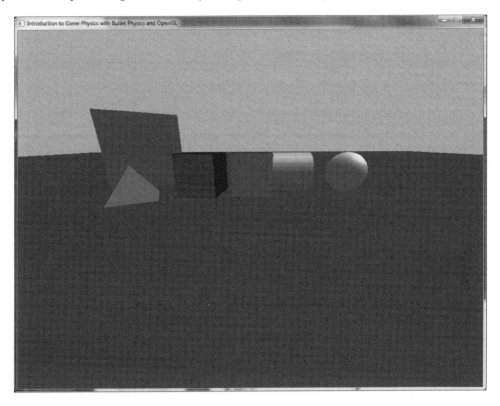

An important point to note before we move on is that Bullet assumes the center of mass of the object is at (0,0,0) relative to the given points, ergo the points must be defined around that location. If we wish to set the center of mass to a different location, then we must call the `setCenterOfMassTransform()` function on the object's rigid body.

Creating convex hulls from mesh data

Building a convex hull by manually typing in the vertex data can be incredibly tedious. So Bullet provides methods for loading customized mesh file data into the desired vertex format that we used earlier, provided the data has been stored in the .obj format (a common format that every 3D modeling tool supports these days). To see this process in action, check out the App_ConvexDecompositionDemo application in the Bullet source code.

However, be warned that creating convex hulls from a complex shape (such as a table or a four-legged chair) requires a lot of CPU cycles to generate accurate collision responses for them. It is wise to stick with simple collision shapes that estimate the physical object, such as boxes and spheres, unless absolutely necessary.

Compound shapes

Bullet also allows us to build another type of customized physics object by combining multiple child shapes together into a parent compound shape.

Continue from here using the Chapter7.3_ CompoundShapes project files.

Compound shapes are treated much the same way as any other shape, except its constituent pieces are stuck together by a set of very rigid constraints (much like the constraints we explored in *Chapter 5, Raycasting and Constraints*). We'll use compound shapes to create a dumbbell, a pair of spheres connected via a connecting rod.

Note that the child shapes do not need to touch one another for the compound shape feature to work. The child shapes could be separated by great distances and still behave as if they were tightly coupled.

The class in question is the btCompoundShape class. The member function addChildShape(), attaches the given child shape into the compound shape at the given transform. Therefore a simple compound shape can be built as follows:

```
// create two shapes for the rod and the load
btCollisionShape* pRod = new btBoxShape(btVector3(1.5f, 0.2f,
  0.2f));
btCollisionShape* pLoad = new btSphereShape(0.5f);
// create a transform we'll use to set each object's position
  btTransform trans;
```

```
trans.setIdentity();
// create our compound shape
btCompoundShape* pCompound = new btCompoundShape();
// add the rod
pCompound->addChildShape(trans, pRod);
trans.setOrigin(btVector3(-1.75f, 0.0f, 0.0f));
// add the top load
pCompound->addChildShape(trans, pLoad);
trans.setIdentity();
// add the bottom load
trans.setOrigin(btVector3(1.75f, 0.0f, 0.0f));
pCompound->addChildShape(trans, pLoad);
// create a game object using the compound shape
CreateGameObject(pCompound, 2.0f, btVector3(0.8,0.4,0.1),
  btVector3(-4, 10.0f, 0.0f));
```

Bullet lets us create yet another complex physics object with only a handful of instructions. But, yet again, we have the problem of rendering this shape. We can use the compound shape's member functions getNumChildShapes(), getChildTransform(), and getChildShape() to iterate through the child shapes, but remember that our DrawShape() command only accepts a single shape to draw at a time, and if we push our compound shape into a game object and render it, it would not draw anything, because the parent itself is not one of the supported types.

What we must do is to call the DrawShape() function recursively for each child as follows:

```
case COMPOUND_SHAPE_PROXYTYPE:
{
  // get the shape
  const btCompoundShape* pCompound = static_cast<const
    btCompoundShape*>(pShape);
  // iterate through the children
  for (int i = 0; i < pCompound->getNumChildShapes(); ++i) {
    // get the transform of the sub-shape
    btTransform thisTransform = pCompound->getChildTransform(i);
    btScalar thisMatrix[16];
    thisTransform.getOpenGLMatrix(thisMatrix);
    // call drawshape recursively for each child. The matrix
    // stack takes care of positioning/orienting the object for us
    DrawShape(thisMatrix, pCompound->getChildShape(i), color);
  }
  break;
}
```

If the purpose of the matrix stack wasn't clear earlier, then the preceding exercise might help. When the two weights of the dumbbell are drawn, it might appear that the only transform information given are the positions at (-1.75,0,0) or (1.75,0,0), and yet it doesn't always render at those exact world space coordinates.

In reality, it renders at the above location relative to the parent object. But why? This powerful mechanism is achieved by adding the child's transformation matrix to the stack (with another call to glPushMatrix()) rendering the child, removing its transform from the stack (with another call to glPopMatrix()), and repeating for the next child. Thus, wherever the parent's transform begins, the matrix stack ensures that the children are always drawn relative to that starting location.

Our application now features our new dumbbell object:

Our new dumbbell object

It's worth mentioning that we only created two unique shapes in memory for our dumbbell: one for the rod and one for the load. Yet, our dumbbell is built from three unique shapes. This is an essential memory saving feature of collision shapes. Their data can be shared by more than one collision object, and still be treated as two unique instances.

Summary

We have created four new types of Bullet collision shapes in our application by introducing more case statements to our `DrawShape()` function. Any object can be built from primitive shapes such as triangles, quads, and so on (which is why they're called primitives), but we have also discovered that there are helper functions inside FreeGLUT called quadrics which make this process easier for us.

In the next chapter, we will explore how collision filtering can be used to develop interesting physics behavior and game logic.

8
Collision Filtering

Collision filtering is an act of informing the physics engine to ignore collisions between specific types of objects. This could either be an optimization to minimize physics processing activity, or an essential component of gameplay. Either way, the mechanism to implement this in Bullet is the same, and we will explore how to implement such a system in this chapter using groups and masks

Groups and masks

The code to implement collision filtering is absolutely trivial, but it requires a good amount of explanation before it can be fully appreciated and understood.

 Continue from here using the `Chapter8_CollisionFiltering` project files.

When we call the `addRigidBody()` function on our world object, there is an overloaded version of the same function with two more parameters that we can input:

- A `short` representing the object's collision group
- A `short` representing the object's collision mask

Each object in our world can be a part of zero, one, or more collision groups. Groups could represent concepts such as players, power-ups, projectiles, enemies, and so on. Meanwhile, the collision mask indicates which groups this object should collide with. In this way, we can use collision filtering to generate an essential element of gameplay logic by preventing the player from being hit by their own weapon projectiles, or preventing enemies from being able to pick up power-ups.

Bullet treats the `short` values as a list of bit flags, and uses simple bitwise operations to perform tests on them. If bitwise operators and bitmasks sound scary or confusing, then this would be a good moment to break open your computer science manual of choice and do a little brush up on the subject. They are a commonly used tool in C++ programming. So common in fact, that we have already used them three times throughout this book in functions such as `glutInitDisplayMode()`, `glutClear()`, and our `DebugDrawer` class.

Bitmasks are used by Bullet for these operations because performing comparisons on them is absurdly fast and they use a minimal amount of data. With potentially thousands of comparisons to perform per simulation step, this is a very worthwhile optimization that has been built into Bullet.

Because the two values for group and mask are `short`s, we have 2 bytes, or 16 bits, to work with. But, Bullet reserves one of these bits for internal usage, which gives us access to the remaining 15, however this should be more than enough groups for most situations.

The last thing to consider is that if we want two objects to collide with one another, then both of their masks must include the group of the opposing object. For example, if we want the players to collide with power-ups, we can set the player's mask to do so; but power-ups must also be flagged to collide with player's, or else the collisions will not occur. Remember this when attempting to use this feature in the future, because it is an easy thing to forget.

The `BasicDemo` application is becoming cluttered, so we have created a specific application to test collision filtering named `CollisionFilteringDemo`. Using this object, instead of `BasicDemo`, required a handful of changes to our `main()` function.

To implement collision filtering, we simply pass the two aforementioned `short`s into our call to the `addRigidBody()` function. This merely requires a change in the parameters and the function calls of `CreateGameObject()`. Because it is so trivial, we won't show the whole source code here, but we will make a couple of relevant points:

```
enum CollisionGroups {
  COLGROUP_NONE = 0,
  COLGROUP_STATIC = 1 << 0,
  COLGROUP_BOX = 1 << 1,
  COLGROUP_SPHERE = 1 << 2
};
```

This `enum`, found in `BulletOpenGLApplication.h`, defines the possible collision groups for our object. Each represents a different group and is represented by a value of 1, but bit shifted left by gradually increasing values of 2, 4, 8, 16, and so on. This is a simple pattern to ensure that each value consumes a unique bit. The same `enum` that defines the values for the groups is also used to determine each new object's collision mask. To set more than one group for an object's collision mask, we use the bitwise-or operator, as follows:

```
COLGROUP_BOX | COLGROUP_STATIC
```

Passing this value as the object's mask makes it collide with any object flagged for either of these groups.

Defining linear and angular freedom

It's becoming increasingly common these days to see the games that are visually 3D, but all gameplay and physics occurs in only two dimensions. These types of games are typically referred to as **2.5D games**. These are either attempts to bring a classic 2D game back to life with modern 3D graphics, or a way to keep the simplicity of 2D gameplay, but give them more life and believability through advanced graphics. To achieve this, physics objects must only be able to move in the X and Y axes, and only able to rotate around the Z axis.

Restrictions of this kind can be applied to any rigid body object in Bullet by setting the linear or angular factor of a rigid body. Simply call the `setLinearFactor()` or `setAngularFactor()` functions on any rigid body, passing in a `btVector3` that specifies which axes are allowed, and which are not. For instance, to restrict the movement of an object to behave as if it was a 2.5D game, we would call:

```
pBody->setLinearFactor(btVector3(1,1,0));
pBody->setAngularFactor(btVector3(0,0,1));
```

To demonstrate this feature, this chapter's source code sets the spheres to only move in the X - Y plane (up/down/left/right relative to our camera's starting position), while being constricted along the Z plane (they cannot move towards/away from the camera's starting position). Even if another object (such as a box we shoot with a right-click) collides with one of the spheres along the Z axis, it still cannot move in that direction. The following call restricts the linear motion of the sphere in such a fashion:

```
pSphere->GetRigidBody()->setLinearFactor(btVector3(1, 1, 0));
```

The `CollisionFilteringDemo` application creates 25 boxes and 25 spheres in a stacked 5 x 5 grid formation. It then configures both types of objects to collide with the ground plane, but also configures such that the boxes cannot collide with the spheres, and vice versa.

When we launch this application, we should observe two stacks of boxes and spheres, each occupying the same space without any collisions between them. There can be collisions only with the objects of the same shape. The following screenshot shows the collision filtering in effect:

Note that the default values for group and mask are set to -1 in the declaration of the CreateGameObject() function. If we remember our signed-integer representations, a value of -1 means every bit is set to 1. Thus, the default values for group and mask make the object a member of every group, and has a mask enabled for every group. This is the reason why the ground plane and our shootable boxes are able to collide with both the boxes and spheres.

Summary

We've explored the power and simplicity of Bullet's collision filtering system, and implemented it into our scene to avoid generating collisions between objects of different groups. This feature can be extended further to all kinds of useful situations, both for the sake of gameplay and for simulation optimization.

In the next chapter, we will explore one final and powerful feature of the Bullet library: Soft bodies!

Soft Body Dynamics

9

Soft bodies are an alternate type of collision object to rigid bodies; they deform as a result of collisions and that allows us to simulate objects made from soft and malleable materials. In this chapter, we will be exploring the nuances of soft body physics and adding a soft body to our scene.

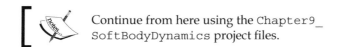 Continue from here using the `Chapter9_ SoftBodyDynamics` project files.

Soft body requirements

One way to think of soft bodies is having a non-rigid constraint on each vertex. When one vertex is moved, the rest move with it, but not to the same extent, and each tries to maintain their distance from their nearest neighbors, or in other words, maintain their original pose. Thus, with a robust constraint system in place (like Bullet has), the mathematics of soft bodies is essentially a larger scale version of the same concept. There's a lot more that goes into the soft body physics simulation, but we don't need a PHD in theoretical physics to add one to our simulation.

The `btSoftRigidDynamicsWorld` world object is required for soft body simulation. This is a requirement since soft bodies are much more mathematically complex than rigid bodies, and so an entirely different world is required to perform the work necessary to move them through space and simulate them correctly.

In addition, this world also requires a slightly different collision configuration object called `btSoftBodyRigidBodyCollisionConfiguration`, and an extra object called `btSoftBodyWorldInfo` is an added attachment onto the soft body worlds, which performs some extra initialization for our world to function.

[Note that this chapter's source code uses a `SoftBodyDemo` application to specifically test this feature.]

Finally, because of the complexity of soft bodies, an entire project/library file must be included in the project in order to compile and launch the application with soft bodies. We must add the `BulletSoftBody` project, and the `BulletSoftBody_vs2010_debug.lib` file.

Initialization

Initialization of the world and collision configuration for soft bodies are not particularly special.

```
m_pCollisionConfiguration = new
  btSoftBodyRigidBodyCollisionConfiguration();
m_pWorld = new btSoftRigidDynamicsWorld(m_pDispatcher,
  m_pBroadphase, m_pSolver, m_pCollisionConfiguration);
```

These calls are identical to the calls used earlier, except using new class types (with much longer names). The most significant change to the soft body world initialization is with the `btSoftBodyWorldInfo` object:

```
btSoftBodyWorldInfo m_softBodyWorldInfo;
m_softBodyWorldInfo.m_dispatcher = m_pDispatcher;
m_softBodyWorldInfo.m_broadphase = m_pBroadphase;
m_softBodyWorldInfo.m_sparsesdf.Initialize();
```

Suffice it to say that this object simply needs the pointers for the collision dispatcher and broad phase objects, and must have it's **Signed Distance Field (SDF** for short) initialized so that it can generate proper collision detection for the world's soft bodies. Diving into the guts of soft bodies could take forever; there are entire volumes of scientific papers on the subject, so we will only be giving concepts such as SDFs a very cursory examination.

The SDF is a data structure that generates a more simplified (sparse) version of the soft body for collision detection in order to improve processing time, and is used to detect the distances between the soft body and other objects. After initialization, it will actively communicate with the dispatcher and the broad phase to generate collision responses for soft bodies (hence it needed the pointers to them).

Creating soft bodies

To create a soft body, we will utilize btSoftBodyHelpers, which contains many useful functions to simplify the act of generating these complex objects. We will use CreateEllipsoid() to build a sphere of triangles (an ellipsoid with equal dimensions is just a sphere), and then configure it with some additional commands. We won't be using GameObject for this object, because CreateEllipsoid() already generates the entire object for us.

```
btSoftBody* pSoftBody =
  btSoftBodyHelpers::CreateEllipsoid
  (m_softBodyWorldInfo,btVector3(0,0,0),btVector3(3,3,3),128);
m_pSoftBodyWorld->addSoftBody(pSoftBody);
```

As with rigid bodies and constraints, we need to specifically add a soft body to the scene before it shows up. This is accomplished by calling the addSoftBody() function on our world object. But, before we attach it, we need to perform some additional initialization.

A soft body is (obviously) not a very rigid structure. It deforms as it collides with other objects. But, the question is how does it deform? What is this object's resistance to being crushed? What is it's ability to maintain its own shape when sitting stationary? How heavy is the entire volume? How much friction does it suffer when morphing and rolling over surfaces? These are all the variables that can be tweaked in any given soft body, making them the most complex type of collision shape that can be found in a Bullet.

The two key values that we can set are the soft body's volume conservation coefficient and it's linear stiffness. Each of these values affects a specific property of the soft body, altering how well it maintains its original shape as it moves and collides with other objects.

```
// set the 'volume conservation coefficient'
pSoftBody->m_cfg.kVC = 0.5;
// set the 'linear stiffness'
pSoftBody->m_materials[0]->m_kLST = 0.5;
```

 Note that m_materials is an array of different materials, which can be assigned to different sections of the same soft body if desired. Make sure that you manipulate it keeping this is mind.

The remaining initialization for our soft body comes through the `setTotalMass()` and `setPose()` functions. As we might expect, `setTotalMass()` simply sets the mass of the soft body, but it also has a profound effect on how the object deforms when it collides with other objects. If we want our shootable boxes to distort the soft body, its mass needs to be relatively low. If we want it to ignore them, then we should set the mass very high.

Finally, `setPose()` is used to generate the necessary constraints of the soft body, telling it to maintain the current pose in which its constituent vertices are positioned. This function takes two booleans, determining if the soft body should attempt to maintain its volume and frame, respectively; each has a significant effect on how the soft body moves.

```
// set the total mass of the soft body
pSoftBody->setTotalMass(5);
// tell the soft body to initialize and
// attempt to maintain the current pose
pSoftBody->setPose(true,false);
```

Rendering soft bodies

Our base application doesn't know anything about soft bodies (nor should it), so we will need to extend the `RenderScene()` function to handle our soft body rendering code. We make use of `btSoftBodyHelpers` again, which contains a function that will help us render our soft body through the very same rendering code that we use to draw the debug lines on the screen. This will require us to add one more function override in our debug drawer to render triangles in addition to lines.

Because our soft body is not built from `GameObject`, we need to handle its rendering a little differently than before. We can obtain and iterate through any soft bodies in our scene by calling the `getSoftBodyArray()` function on our world object and then use our debug drawer to render each of its triangles:

```
// check the list of our world's soft bodies
for (int i=0; i< m_pSoftBodyWorld->getSoftBodyArray().size(); i++)
  {
  // get the body
  btSoftBody*  pBody = (btSoftBody*)m_pSoftBodyWorld-
    >getSoftBodyArray()[i];
  // is it possible to render?
```

```
if (m_pSoftBodyWorld->getDebugDrawer() && !(m_pSoftBodyWorld-
  >getDebugDrawer()->getDebugMode() &
    (btIDebugDraw::DBG_DrawWireframe))) {
  // draw it
  btSoftBodyHelpers::Draw(pBody, m_pSoftBodyWorld-
    >getDebugDrawer(), m_pSoftBodyWorld->getDrawFlags());
  }
}
```

Launching our application now, we should observe a sphere fall, collide with the ground, and deform. We can also launch boxes with the right-mouse button to deform it even more. The following screenshot shows our soft body falling from the sky and deforming under its own weight:

 Note that we cannot pick up and move this object with the left-mouse button because it is not a rigid body, and our picking code exits only if it detects so (otherwise it would crash!).

Soft bodies are very complex objects with a lot of mathematics behind them. Consequently, they are processor intensive, and there are many values that can be tweaked to generate the desired effect. This data can be accessed through the following two member variables of the soft body object: m_cfg and m_materials.

To see more interesting scenarios involving soft bodies, check out the App_SoftBody demo in Bullet's demo applications.

Summary

In this chapter, we have taken an introductory look at soft body physics, and several helper functions that can provide more advanced functionality if needed. There is much more that can be done with these interesting objects, and there are even more features that the Bullet library offers us, but regrettably we must begin wrapping up the book and leaving behind some closing thoughts.

All that's left is to say is farewell and good luck with your future game development projects. There's always more to learn and understand about game development, which makes it a very tough field to work in and keep pace with. But, for many of us, we wouldn't want it any other way, because if it was easy it would be boring!

We hope that you've learned a great deal about the fundamentals of game physics and graphics with this book, and have the drive to continue learning everything you need to bring your awesome game ideas to life!

Index

R

Raycast() function 66, 88
raycasting 63
  picking rays 64, 65
RemovePickingConstraint() function 72

S

scene
  rendering 19
setAngularFactor() function 101
setDebugDrawer() function 58
setLinearVelocity() function 65
setParam() function 71
setPose() function 106
setTotalMass() function 106
shaders 33
ShootBox() command 83
ShootBox() function 64
simulation
  stopping 47, 48
Single Instruction, Multiple
    Data (SIMD) 55
soft body
  creating 105
  initialization 104
  rendering 106, 107
  requisites 103, 104
specular lighting 28
Spiral of Death 60
Standard Template Library (STL) 54, 77
stepSimulation() function 48, 60

T

torques 82
transform data
  rendering from 47
trigger volumes
  building 80
  contact response, disabling 81, 82

U

UpdateCamera() 34
user input
  gathering 35

V

vertex cloud 91

W

W key 82
wrappers 8

Z

z-buffer 29

Thank you for buying
Learning Game Physics with Bullet Physics and OpenGL

About Packt Publishing

Packt, pronounced 'packed', published its first book "*Mastering phpMyAdmin for Effective MySQL Management*" in April 2004 and subsequently continued to specialize in publishing highly focused books on specific technologies and solutions.

Our books and publications share the experiences of your fellow IT professionals in adapting and customizing today's systems, applications, and frameworks. Our solution based books give you the knowledge and power to customize the software and technologies you're using to get the job done. Packt books are more specific and less general than the IT books you have seen in the past. Our unique business model allows us to bring you more focused information, giving you more of what you need to know, and less of what you don't.

Packt is a modern, yet unique publishing company, which focuses on producing quality, cutting-edge books for communities of developers, administrators, and newbies alike. For more information, please visit our website: www.packtpub.com.

About Packt Open Source

In 2010, Packt launched two new brands, Packt Open Source and Packt Enterprise, in order to continue its focus on specialization. This book is part of the Packt Open Source brand, home to books published on software built around Open Source licences, and offering information to anybody from advanced developers to budding web designers. The Open Source brand also runs Packt's Open Source Royalty Scheme, by which Packt gives a royalty to each Open Source project about whose software a book is sold.

Writing for Packt

We welcome all inquiries from people who are interested in authoring. Book proposals should be sent to author@packtpub.com. If your book idea is still at an early stage and you would like to discuss it first before writing a formal book proposal, contact us; one of our commissioning editors will get in touch with you.

We're not just looking for published authors; if you have strong technical skills but no writing experience, our experienced editors can help you develop a writing career, or simply get some additional reward for your expertise.

OpenGL Development Cookbook

ISBN: 978-1-849695-04-6   Paperback: 326 pages

Over 40 recipes to help you learn, understand, and implement mondern OpenGL in your applications

1. Explores current graphics programming techniques including GPU-based methods from the outlook of modern OpenGL 3.3

2. Includes GPU-based volume rendering algorithms

3. Discover how to employ GPU-based path and ray tracing

Cocos2d for iPhone 1 Game Development Cookbook

ISBN: 978-1-849514-00-2   Paperback: 446 pages

Over 90 recipes for iOS 2D game development using cocos2d

1. Discover advanced Cocos2d, OpenGL ES, and iOS techniques spanning all areas of the game development process

2. Learn how to create top-down isometric games, side-scrolling platformers, and games with realistic lighting

3. Full of fun and engaging recipes with modular libraries that can be plugged into your project

Please check **www.PacktPub.com** for information on our titles

Box2D for Flash Games

ISBN: 978-1-849519-62-5   Paperback: 166 pages

Create amazing and realistic physics-based Flash games using Box2D

1. Design blockbuster physics game and handle every kind of collision

2. Build and destroy levels piece by piece

3. Create vehicles and bring them to life with motors

3D Game Development with Microsoft Silverlight 3: Beginner's Guide

ISBN: 978-1-847198-92-1   Paperback: 452 pages

A practical guide to creating real-time responsive online 3D games in Silverlight 3 using C#, XBAP WPF, XAML, Balder, and Farseer Physics Engine

1. Develop online interactive 3D games and scenes in Microsoft Silverlight 3 and XBAP WPF

2. Integrate Balder 3D engine 1.0, Farseer Physics Engine 2.1, and advanced object-oriented techniques to simplify the game development process

3. Enhance development with animated 3D characters, sounds, music, physics, stages, gauges, and backgrounds

Please check **www.PacktPub.com** for information on our titles

Printed in Great Britain
by Amazon